Religion as Critique

Religion as Critique

Robert John Ackermann

The University of Massachusetts Press   Amherst, 1985

Copyright © 1985 by
The University of Massachusetts Press
All rights reserved
Printed in the United States of America

Library of Congress Cataloging in Publication Data
Ackermann, Robert John, 1933-
Religion as critique.
Bibliography: p.
Includes index.
1. Religion. I. Title.
BL48.A26   1985   200'.1   84-16471
ISBN 0-87023-462-5
ISBN 0-87023-463-3 (pbk.)

To My Parents

Who taught me to read, play the piano, and think for myself. In the absence of these cultivated abilities, I am sure that I would have been a miserable adult. Although this is not the work of a theologian, perhaps it will be a suitable expression of gratitude.

Contents

Preface   ix

Introduction   1

1   Defining Religion   5

2   Major Contemporary Theologies   29

3   Religion and Social Issues   55

4   Grid, Group, and Religion   83

5   Civil Religion in the United States   113

Notes   145

Bibliography   161

Index   169

*Although people like to hear that they
and the universe are good and getting
better all the time, they like even more to
be told that they are wicked sinners in
a dark pit, and can only be saved through
great effort, the repetition of magic
formulae, and the aid of invisible beings.*
—*Alison Lurie*, Imaginary Friends

Preface

THIS BOOK is written partly out of exasperation at the sheer dullness of the philosophy of religion. To examine the logical structure of textual arguments is to miss everything that has made religion alive to people in the past. Religions have arisen as legitimate protests against societies and ways of life, providing in the process the overpowering foundations for laying down one's life to improve the lot of humanity. From successful protest, of course, comes eventual orthodoxy, and perhaps even decline and death. Logical structure cannot deal with these historical themes.

I have looked at some major religious traditions that still influence current events as though they were both dead and alive, dead in their orthodoxy, but alive in providing a source of critical ideas for evaluating surrounding society. Recent events have shown religious cultists as kooks who need, possibly, police immolation to preserve the order of surrounding society. Recent events are thus an ironic measure of the potential power of religious protest. Religious ideas can make one pretty angry about surrounding society, and may tempt one into incivility, which, as we shall see, is a cardinal sin of the current civil religion in the United States. In exonerating religion from the charge of intellectual vacuity by attempting to point to its critical moment, no attempt is being made to justify violence based on religious scruples, certainly no general justification. But the important matter is to speak out against a monoculture whose resources are too impoverished to provide more than short-term social steering. This is the historical mode of prophecy, and it must entail some risks.

The subtle impact of Durkheim on religious studies is hardly ended. Where Americans are, in some sense there America is also, as follows from Durkheim's reflections. A room therefore does not contain just furniture and people. All religious traditions have known this and religion in America is no exception. Where religion seems to deny transcendence, as in some of its current forms, the denial itself implicitly recognizes this, and is only an opposing dogma concerning values. Durkheim, or Mary Douglas, can develop reflective theories of religion, because the elementary forms of religious life that they scrutinize have achieved an equilibrium with surrounding society. What will be argued here is that religious structure can become anachronistic with respect to surrounding society, forcing change, and providing the basis for social critique. A religion opposes an ideal structure to an actual society, allowing always for the possibility of criticism, a possibility heightened when anachronism is patent.

Cutting through the fog laid about in the apparent service of religion are a few thunderbolts. In my own case, books by Robert Bellah, John Cuddihy, Mary Douglas, and Thomas Luckmann have brought me outright excitement coupled with some peace of mind, some idea that I have finally grasped the location of a few solid landmarks for reflection on these matters.

For philosophers, this study may seem a pile of assertions without supporting arguments. I'm tempted to suggest that this is also the structure of many philosophical classics, but I will content myself with observing that the logical criticism of theological arguments that dominates the discussions in the philosophy of religion simply isn't relevant to what is at stake in viewing religion as critique. In the past, philosophers have drawn on religious images as a source of critique of social or even philosophical systems. This is a form of criticism that can be as rigorous as noting invalidities in argument, although the object of criticism is completely different, and greater risks may be entailed in the effort. Specific criticisms themselves are not advanced here; rather a study of the space in which they can be advanced on the basis of religious values. The analysis of religious argument can stop well short of social criticism; I am arguing here that religion as critique and a philosophy of religion associated with such a critique cannot ultimately exercise the same self-restraint.

For sociologists, this study may seem to ignore the diverse sociological studies of religion in the United States. No comprehensive analysis of sociological studies is undertaken, but this is by design. The studies in question look at belief structures in the current conceptual framework, and on this basis they can contribute to an understanding of the growth of internalized religion, and the current religious situation. But as these studies have defined relevant belief against the dogmas of the institutionalized churches, they frequently ask questions that are off to one side from the point of view of religious social critique. I am concerned to advance some hypotheses that can later be formulated in more testable form. My analysis in chapter 5 is based on some previous studies, but, just as important, on my own observations, television watching, and disjointed reading. I remain methodologically convinced that one needs to achieve closure on interesting hypotheses by these means before empirical formulation and confirmatory studies can be brought to bear on them. If the arguments of this book are correct, existing surveys generally ask irrelevant questions with respect to the issues at stake in religious critique.

For all readers, there will be stretches of exposition that are both eclectic and loose. I intend to be sketching out some facts that are meant to motivate the major lines of argument, without discussing too many details. In order to keep things under control, the Introduction and Chapter Analyses should be carefully read along with the text, since the major claims are clearly stated there, and are not constantly repeated in the chapter material. This will also allow the knowledgeable reader to skim some of the expository material, especially in chapters 2 and 3, without losing track of the major lines of argument. For other readers, the expository sections may serve as reminders of the range of information on which the central claims are based, or even serve as an introduction to this information.

It is common to thank people in the Preface for help and constructive criticism, but most readers of the first form of the manuscript were disturbed by its deviance from normal scholarship in this area, and would perhaps be made uncomfortable by association with it. Many objected to the inclusion of Marxism as a religion, in spite of the fact that its religious forms are clearly evident, and that its inclusion simplifies theorizing concerning the relationship of religion to society considerably. If one wants to believe that there are "scientific" forms of Marxism as well, nothing contained in this study precludes that possibility. In spite of this observation, I may serve my friends better in many cases by not explicitly naming them, avoiding for them through public silence the risk of contamination by association with those ideas that they would not choose to acknowledge as congruent with their own. They have my gratitude, nonetheless, for providing sporadic conversation on diverse topics. My gratitude is also extended to those (hopefully) kindred spirits acknowledged in the footnotes. Phenomenologically speaking, this has been a fairly lonely path of inquiry, although I should like to expressly thank several people. First, an anonymous referee of an earlier version provided sensitive but devastating criticisms that enabled me to considerably improve the manuscript. Should this be noticed by that referee, I hope that my opinion about improvement will prove pleasing. Second, I am very grateful for Richard Martin's handling of the manuscript, and I hope that his anticipations of critical response will prove accurate. Third, my thanks to "Thunderbolt," who lifted my spirits twice, the second time just when it was most needed.

Amherst, Massachusetts
April 1983

Introduction

THIS BOOK has had to cut a crude path through thickets of controversy; otherwise the argument would have been swallowed up in the jungle of religious studies. The path is not entirely new; many have traveled at least stretches of it before—but it needs to be mapped out clearly in our time. Religion is a perennial source of social critique, but religion in general is not equivalent to social critique. What will be argued here by an assemblage of reminders is that the major religions always retain the potential of developing pungent social critique, no matter how accommodating a form they have assumed in particular institutional contexts. If religion is to provide the possibility of social critique, it can never be reduced to a set of mechanically understood dogmata, for in that form it would necessarily lose touch with changing social reality. Anyone who studies religion will have this thought. The history of Christianity, for example, indicates critique of society in both the Old Testament prophets and the New Testament epistles, and the emergence of Christianity in the Roman Empire, as well as the emergence of radical Protestantism in the Reformation, is sufficient to recall strong critique of surrounding society that has intensified with revolutionary consequences at particular moments of historical times. Critique does not exhaust religion, but religion that cannot critique is already dead.

Perhaps this point will be considered noncontroversial on reflection, but it is essential to secure it if the philosophy of religion is to find interesting subject matter in our time. Study of the forms of religious social critique is quite different from study of the logic of religious argument, or the sociology of existing religious adherence. The subject matter to be sketched here is not to be found by either of these approaches, but it is necessary to resuscitate it as background for an understanding of why people should ever feel driven to accept what may seem logically dubious positions, or why they should distort their lives for what seems to others mere dogma. Necessity is heightened by the current religious situation, in which religion in large populations may seem to be taking on forms that deliberately minimize the complexity of religious belief, making critique more difficult to achieve as internal criticism. The largest power blocs in the contemporary world can be associated with secular religions that are more consistent than medieval Catholicism or emergent Protestantism, but at the same time are less powerful as generators of critique. In the case of both blocs, civil and religious accommodation have resulted in religions of stunted self-critical potential. This situation is new, as is the institutional isolation of denominational churches associated with it, and it must be studied as part of a study of religion as critique.

We will concentrate here on the critical potential for Christianity in the United States, since the personal experiences of presumed readers will be relevant to an evaluation of the rather bold historical claims that are asserted later. Again, mere reminders will suffice to establish the essential role of religious critique in the founding of the Colonies, and the complex interpenetration of sacred and secular values enmeshed with the performance of both private and public duties in colonial settings. The separation of church and state, coupled with legally supported religious pluralism, gradually produced a separation of religious ideologies. In the case of many particular individuals, a complicated secular/sacred tangle became separated into two religions, and two sets of associated values. The separate secular religion that resulted required its own legitimacy. This fact has sometimes been partially noticed by scholars on the model of institutional religion and the religion called a civil religion, but it will be argued here that the extent of this religion exceeds what can be noticed on this model. Some of the legitimacy of the secular civil religion originated in older sacred values which were at first associated with the new secular religion. Civility and individual responsibility for the conduct of one's own life, central features of the new religion, could at first be associated with Christian virtues. In time, however, the sacred aura was transferred to the new virtues, and the older values eroded. The other religion emerging from the separation, a privatized legacy of the virtues of Christian community and caring, not overtly embodying the social critique that had passed over to the secular religion, gradually lost social significance to the secular religion, the latter becoming buttressed epistemologically by a solidifying scientific consensus. Institutional churches became largely irrelevant as organized centers of social critique during this process, adopting commodity forms of religion supportive and therapeutic with respect to surrounding society. Religion became largely invisible in the denominational churches, as Luckmann has observed.[1] In the latter part of the book we will attempt an examination of the secular religion that remains outside the churches as a result of this process of change. The critical potential of religion in confrontation with this secular version will be nearly obvious. This is not a history of social change. What is observed here to have taken place is judged by an examination of the starting point and the current situation. A historical examination would require a complex look at different churches and different regions, something that would blur the outlines of the path being cleared in this study.

The arguments advanced here accept the old generalization that every society has an integrating religion, but it doesn't accept functionalist arguments because it also cedes to religion the power of disruption.[2] We are attempting simply to locate the religions that the generalization postulates. In the case of Eastern power blocs, this is accomplished by taking an appropriate form of Marxism as the religion. In the case of Western power blocs, the analysis becomes complicated, as a secular religion is to be discovered here

of more pervasive and ominous dimensions than those previously
sketched out in the literature. To locate this American secular religion, I have not looked to institutions, but have attempted to utilize
various ideas of Mary Douglas about how feelings of aversion or
revulsion can provide clues to deep-lying religious values.[3] The
argument is that people haven't become less religious, but that they
have been overtly offered less interesting religions, religions whose
critical potential is blunted by accommodation to secular power.
Both blocs, so to speak, have religions that still contain the vestiges
of ideas that can produce self-critique, but these ideas seem played
out in public. Thus it is no surprise that major internal criticisms are
taken from Marxism in the West, and Christianity in the East, re-
peating the old strategy of looking for critical ideas in a locally
untainted or uncorrupted source. This hardly precludes the attempt
at internal criticism by appeal to an earlier form of the local tradition, as the attempt by the New Right in the United States to re-
vivify what is seen as an earlier version of Christianity for the
purposes of social steering indicates. What tells against these attempts is that the earlier forms can't be exactly recaptured, as the
separated civil religion has carried with it some of the old values,
and then leached them out. Intervening history is thus a subtle but
inescapable indication of what can go wrong. Attention to such
structural problems of religious critique cannot properly be undertaken until views about the history of religion as critique have been
sharpened and thrashed out, the task to which this discussion has
been directed.

I

Defining Religion

CHAPTER ANALYSIS   Any attempt to define religion in the conceptual space of current analytical philosophy must confront the
fact that religion is seen in contrast to science, the two dealing with
divergent domains, but in this contrast science is given all the positive epistemological markers. As a result, religion must inevitably
be seen as epistemologically inferior to science and as the bearer of
inconsistency and irrationality from a scientific point of view. This
situation and its consequences are explored here in terms of the
existing literature, and it is observed that only trivial conceptions of
religion are possible given this way of initiating discussion. Rather
than taking religion as a set of beliefs about some domain distinct
from that of science, it will be argued that religion is a source of pictures of how the world ought to be, pictures that can be repeatedly
reinterpreted to evaluate new and even unexpected social patterns.
The longevity of religion is related to its continuing ability to adapt
its highest level pictures to new situations and new forms of critique. Consistent scientific pictures of the world are intended to be
refuted as quickly as possible, so that better pictures can be derived.
Refutation of a religion, were that possible, would leave a society
without the conceptual resources to deal with novel situations. This
is one reason why religions do not exist merely as collections of
dogmata. In science, pictures of how the world is get refuted and

replaced, while in religion, pictures of how the world should be become reinterpreted to assess society as it is. That the pictures stay in place and provide new criteria is part of the phenomenology of religion, which takes them as imposed by some superior force in order to legitimate their retention. Viewing religion as critique allows us to see that religion and science are not similar discourses over different domains at some primitive epistemological level. A religion, if anything, is more analogous to the set of ideas or concepts that are continuously reutilized in scientific theorizing than it is to a settled formulation of some particular scientific theory. Pursuing this analysis, we shall attempt to draw in later chapters some conclusions concerning the contemporary religious situation in the United States that are made accessible by the notion of religion as critique. This approach offers a conception of the task of the philosophy of religion that has an empirical bite on the social situation of religious belief.

CONTEMPORARY philosophy of religion faces a crisis that at times it seems unaware of. Insofar as philosophers examine the theological texts of various churches, and examine them with an eye toward argumentative structure and logical consistency, they are pursuing a task well suited to the tools of philosophical analysis, but a task that doesn't necessarily deal at all with the presumed focus of concern. There is no necessity for thinking that religion is currently embodied in these texts or these institutions; no more so than for thinking that science is currently embodied in the texts of Sir Isaac Newton or the investigation of nature by isolated individuals. Here we shall begin again, attempting to locate a topic for philosophical discussion of more current relevance than the rationality of theological argument. This preliminary discussion attempts to put limits on a notion of religion whose instantiation in contemporary American culture will occupy us for the rest of this investigation.

A first observation of considerable importance is that religion and science have currently accommodated each other as separate domains; intellectually, textually, and institutionally separate domains. Such a decisive separation is a presupposition of the frequently held discussions about the relationship of science to religion, including those discussions where scientists openly speak of their "religious" views, and where they argue that there is a substantive relationship between their religious views and their scientific views. Historically, we have reached a position where the older notion of natural theology is a harassed and minority option of study. The scientification of the universe is officially (ideologically) complete. Where science and religion could once compromise one another by agreeing that the existence of a creator, or the possibility of the existence of a creator, could be established by a careful reading of the universe, the details of the creator to be supplied by faith, the details of the universe by science, the mystery of the universe now calls simply for more science in most philosophical circles. Scientific knowledge has displaced defeated religious knowledge in common philosophical opinion, and it has become the sole entry to the meaning of the universe.

Let us look a little more closely at these sundered domains. At a superficial level, there are a variety of sciences and a variety of religions, or at least a variety of churches. Scientific variety is subject to ideological smoothing through the hypothesis of the unity of science. This hypothesis is to the effect that there is one universe, and a variety of levels at which it is studied. There is no reason to suppose that these levels can't be brought into conceptual coincidence as science develops, according to this hypothesis, so we can think of science as one institution, with a single task (understanding the universe), just the picture that is needed if science is to be taken as providing sole epistemological access to the truth about the universe. No matter how this picture may be shaken by the impact of recent, more relativistic philosophies of science, this picture of a unified science is definitely part of the phenomenological starting point in contemporary philosophical analysis. Opposed to theoretically unified science is an array of religions which by itself is an epistemological embarrassment to any claims to religious truth. Many of these religions say quite contradictory things about a subject identified as God, and because God is the focus of this attention, and because there is agreement that there is only one God, these positions are manifestly contradictory. Ecumenical movements have looked for common ground, but the form of epistemological stitching together of various levels of investigation exhibited by the unity of science hypothesis is not available to an ecumenism that must deal with the level on which God is said to exist, and with the conflicts on just this level. Science, buttressed by the doctrine of the unity of science, which here plays an ideological rather than a known epistemological role, is the very picture of objective knowledge. Religion, a welter of warring and competing sects, cults, and churches, is the picture of confusion and relativity. The total picture simply depicts and reflects the decisive epistemological victory of science, and the seeming actual position of religion, assigned to the role of object of a personal (subjective) decision, possibly chosen for the purpose of making one feel better. What ridiculous grounds for explaining observed conversion to religion! One couldn't find satisfaction in a conscious choice to be satisfied, since the level of self-deception is too blatant, so this picture leads inevitably to the view that unconscious, irrational factors lead to the acceptance of a religion, which in turn makes one feel better. Something like this must be set in place for religious converts who otherwise appear normal except for the seriousness of their religious conviction. Science and religion are separate, but science becomes the repository of rationality, and this fact forces religion to appear irrational, with a choice of religion perhaps ultimately explicable in the same terms as one's choice of toothpaste in technological society. It may well be that in various instances choice of a church is analogous to the choice of toothpaste as completing an image of self for others, but we are after deeper issues.

Both the philosophy of science and the philosophy of religion are deeply affected by the picture of separate domains. Philosophers of science typically ignore religious belief, or cite it only as an example of nonscientific, irrational belief. Philosophers of religion typically accept the separation, and then argue that religion is epistemologically bankrupt, and rests on an existential choice, or that religion has a different epistemology from science, or that at least some of the epistemological standards of science are also to be found in religion. Most of this analysis is boring, trivial, and predictable, because the picture of a separation between science and religion represented in the theological positions from which the analysis begins means that the discussion inevitably repeats philosophical apologetics for the epistemological superiority of science.

Blatant forms of this situation exist where epistemological standards from science are simply set against religious claims, and it is asked what religious claims could possibly assert from the standpoint of rational epistemology. For example, it can be discovered as the result of analytic forays into religious texts that many propositions about God are not testable, not verifiable, or not falsifiable. One could then draw the conclusion that religious beliefs are not scientific statements about fact, which is, of course, much ado about nothing in view of the presuppositions of the investigation.[1] A somewhat more empirical route to the same end comes from the study of the retention of religious belief in the face of apparent falsification.[2] Suppose members of a sect believe that some important event, say the appearance of a god, will occur at a prophesied time and place. Suppose the appearance apparently fails to take place, as has been observed of such predictions on occasion. Some sects disband or split apart after such occurrences, but attention is directed to those cases where the belief in the authority of the religion is retained. Is this irrational? It is *if* you accept a philosophy of science that precludes a certain kind of a posteriori adjustment of theories to data. Or, it would be *if* the study of the religion hadn't changed the nature of the religion so as to produce the prediction.[3] The logic of the situation simply doesn't determine the rationality of religious belief. The logic of the situation plus some view about the rationality of science or what is established scientific data, background that is all too often assumed without recognition, and all too often assumed because of an assumption about the epistemological authority of science, may lead to the view that religious beliefs are irrational, but the logic of the situation by itself can't establish that religious belief is irrational. And, of course, by the same token, the rationality of religion can't be established by such exercises.

Another approach is to concede rationality to the domain of science, and to argue that religion has completely different epistemological standards, or only shares logical standards of coherence with science. As an example of the former strategy, there are those who adopt Wittgenstein's later philosophy to argue that science and religion are different forms of life, each with a logic immanent to its practice.[4] Only believers can understand belief; the attempt to grasp religion from a (scientific) outside is similar to bad anthropology which judges one culture by the standards of another. The logic of this position is perhaps impregnable, but what a religiously abject and defensive position it describes! It can't begin to explain why some outsider should feel the strength of a religious position, and be drawn to conversion, while others remain unaffected. Those who accept the joint rule of logic are free to argue that the arguments for the existence of God can be studied logically, and so they can, but, in spite of the continually resurgent appeal of the ontological proof of God's existence for philosophers, the end result of discussion is that the proofs aren't valid by logical standards, or, where they are, coercive force requires that some matter of fact be inevitably accepted upon study, and the dubious epistemology of religious belief inserts itself once again.[5]

As with many conceptual distinctions, border crossing examples are likely to be dealt with by summary dismissal. Just as the defense of science to Velikovsky's theories or ESP claims is likely to be summary dismissal without a careful consideration of logic or methodology, attempts to mix science and religion are treated by instant preconception. There is a long history of scientific attack on religion, not without its consequences for the present situation. Francis Galton, in 1872, produced a statistical argument that prayer had no efficacy, based on observations such as Christian sovereigns tend not to be long-lived, in spite of multiple and constant prayers for their longevity.[6] But Galton himself apparently said this tongue-in-cheek, rather more enjoying the potential discomfiture of opponents, than assuming the argument to be fatal to religion. It is rather obvious, as Galton himself knew, that there was no way to show that sovereigns would live to the same age without prayers on their behalf, and there was no way of determining just how sincere the prayers in question were, or how God might have taken them, or even how God might have judged the sovereigns independently of the appeal of prayer. Further, no real attempts were made by either side to carry out exact studies; common assumptions about the outcome of such studies (although not their significance) made that moot in practice. A modern version, of a reverse nature, could be the argument that the very low probability of a complete solar eclipse being visible from Earth indicates that the event cannot be due to chance, but is more likely to be the result of divine planning which has constructed a universe placing people at the center of cosmic drama.[7] Or consider the Shroud of Turin.[8] Scientists have examined it inconclusively, but let us suppose it turned out to be what some think it might be. Well then, some of the Bible *is* a factual account, an embarrassment for some, but a conclusion leaving much hermeneutical ambiguity in the text. These arguments among initiates are mostly for fun, invitations neither seriously issued nor accepted, somewhat like Muhammad Ali's friendly invitations to opponents to join him in the corner of the boxing ring. The nervousness hovering around these matters is a sure sign of an inflexible conceptual boundary.

Now let us consider more closely the positions of philosophical guardians of the border. The work of T. S. Kuhn in the philosophy of science, which had the result in many philosophical circles of locating some religious aspects of authority and faith in the pursuit of normal science, has been greeted by these border guards with summary dismissal of Kuhn as a sociologist (rather than a philosopher) of science, studying the lamentable shortcomings of actual scientists rather than the ideal behavior of totally rational scientists.[9] The border is preserved by emptying science of irrationality and by shifting actual practice into a pragmatic realm of sociology, thus making rationality a defining property of idealized scientific behavior within an analytical model of what scientific practice should be. Religion is then a domain characterized in actual practice by the play of dark and mysterious forces not subject to rational control. This way to deal with the mutual pollution of science and religion in practice is to locate rationality totally in the domain of idealized science, and irrationality totally in the domain of religion. For this purpose, Christian doctrines of the incarnation and the nature of God, set against the visible presence of evil in the world, become a focus of attention. The necessity of believing such doctrine coupled with the epistemological prestige of science then precludes in our time Tertullian's philosophical defense of belief in Christianity which is based on the insouciant observation that belief *requires* the absurdity of religion. Here the quick charge of irrationality has been heard for many years on the basis of some very shoddy reasoning, reasoning that is obviously fallacious unless one happens to believe Christianity so absurd on its face that one's logical acumen is occluded. There is often an observable rush to condemn that is quite curious when set against the public claim that a point of logic is being considered. We will consider this matter only in the context of the problem of evil.

Many philosophers have assumed that God's properties of omniscience, omnipotence, and benevolence are incompatible with the existence of evil in the world.[10] The argument is roughly that if God were benevolent, he would want to eradicate evil, and he could accomplish this through his ability to recognize evil (omniscience) and his powers to accomplish its removal (omnipotence). Yet evil exists. Christianity thus appears to be irrational because it is inconsistent with obvious fact, and it can't be the object of rational belief. If Christianity is contradictory, it can be rejected without worry as false according to logical lights, a possible reason for philosophers to allay anxiety with the quick logical kill. The surface plausibility of incompatibility seems ultimately mistaken, leaving philosophers who accept this plausibility stranded with the view that their desire to find Christianity irrational has clouded their logical powers. To begin with, the informal argument sketched above can't be readily expanded into a formal and valid argument. And it is possible to give a proof of compatibility that meets standards of modern logic.[11] This proof revives the Leibnizian idea that God may not be free to instantiate logically contradictory worlds, and that there are no logically consistent worlds in which there are creatures with free will and no evil. This makes free will the cause of evil, of course, and it does not by itself deal with the question of why the world God instantiated in creating our world needed to include creatures with free will. The argument is that God, in considering whether to instantiate a world with a free creature, always confronts a time where the creature will cause evil if allowed to act freely. Therefore God can prevent evil (by causing the creature to act otherwise) or find free will and evil in the world, but not free will in the absence of evil over the total course of any world. There is, in short, no world with free creatures and no evil, therefore the best possible world that God could instantiate must contain at least some evil. This argument, which seems logically valid within its assumptions, indicates that Christianity can be represented in a consistent version with respect to the problem of evil.

There are other problems with Christianity and logic, such as that posed by the incarnation. In modern versions of Christianity which minimize the divinity of Christ, however, the consistency of the existence of evil with God's nature renders the picture of a logically consistent Christianity within sight. Perhaps all the major religions can meet standards of logical rigor in presenting at least some versions of their claims. This seems, in fact, highly likely. The plausibility of these versions, and of the religions in any version, is a totally different matter, of course. It would seem highly suspect if logic alone should prove capable of defending science's claim to epistemological superiority, and it is time to drop attempts to use it toward that end. Discussion of religion should proceed as though a phenomenon of its magnitude and longevity could present grounds for rational belief once we recognize that religion is not science.

Returning to our discussion of the relationship of science and religion in contemporary philosophy, some attempts to bridge the gap between science and religion in a manner that would utilize science to support religion should also be noted. In pure Protestant theology, the foundational epistemology often associated with positivism's account of science can be copied by relying on direct experience of God, the defense of religion then being that its authentic claims rest on such experience. This may or may not be accompanied by a logical development of ideas, but the skeptic can be countered with the claim that he or she has simply not had the

authenticating experiences. Scientific epistemologists may argue
that this loses the public observability of scientific data, or that such
episodes seem peculiarly self-authenticating, but at least some philosophers of science argue that public observability is the fruition of
a long period of scientific training, a period that might be thought
analogous to a religious meditative regimen, and so the argument is
not conclusive as to the epistemological status of these episodes.
A more recent version of an attempt to find a positive epistemology
for religion can be discerned in attempts to ground mystical states
in split-brain scientific findings.[12] Mystics often tend to sound more
alike, insofar as they can express their claims, than the official
theologies of churches they may be associated with. The integrative
nature of mystical insight could be related to the properties of right-
brain experience in the scientific findings, and some objective basis
for often derided mystical claims located in a common human
physiological potential.[13] But what do altered state experiences
indicate? Insofar as they occur in the natural world, they require
interpretation. Although they may have been unexpected events for
some scientists, there is no reason why they can't be considered
representative of the natural potentialities of the human brain, and
incorporated into scientific psychology. On the other hand, they
may be the locus of an impingement of the transcendent onto the
natural world. By themselves, they are without significance, and
can't settle any issues about the relationship of science and religion.

   Almost all the contemporary philosophical discussion of religion
has proceeded on the basis of a philosophy of language based on
a crude conception of scientific verifiability. If the truth or falsity of
sentences is a matter of their being logically true or false, or of being
functions of observable fact, then one can support a positivistic
conception of scientific truth, and oppose it to nonsense. But the
contextual complexity of language has not really been touched by
philosophical analysis to date. Recently, analysis of propositional
attitudes has been attempted, but such commonplaces as figures of
speech elude a settled science. Waiting in the wings are such phenomena as jokes and myths. Perhaps if scientific theorizing is one
day assimilated to some category of an important kind of fiction

that helps us to understand our world, the present assumptions underlying the split of science and religion will appear crude and unacceptable. But we will make no effort to anticipate such developments here.

To this point, it has been argued that science and religion are most acceptably perceived as separate domains in modern thought, with neither able to impugn the existence of the other on logical grounds, although science has become recognized as the sole source of knowledge about the natural world. This leaves some independent form of religious knowledge as at least a possibility. A strategy of accommodation along these lines has been available for some time. Kierkegaard, for example, saw the philosophical task as that of sketching out consistent attitudes toward life, attitudes associated with different kinds of practical choice, but did not assume that one could argue for or against these options. That would, of course, entail the religious significance of natural fact, and hence run against the difficulties we have already surveyed. From Kierkegaard's point of view, most people pursue confused or paradoxical lives, based on insufficient clarity about the kind of life they are living. When lives are philosophically clarified, a person who wishes a consistent life can only choose from the possible kinds. Kierkegaard's defense of Christianity may permit a consistent style of Protestant inwardness compatible with the separation of science and religion, but it recognizes no social significance for religious belief or perhaps can be said to have a peculiarly detached and distorted attitude toward human social relationships. Kierkegaard's position does not exist without problems, but it is usually ignored or accepted, rather than confronted.[14]

A clear contemporary statement of this situation is to be found in Kolakowski's *Religion*.[15] Here the sacred is perceived as independent of the secular, and religious knowledge as having no support in, nor any consequences for, scientific or secular knowledge. The religious person may resist tyranny longer, or adjust better to personal disaster, but that is unrelated to the *truth* of what is accepted on religious grounds. Kolakowski produces one interesting argument toward describing a relationship between religion and science that does not make their content interdependent.[16] If the secular human being accepts an absolute truth of any kind, accepts that something could not be wrong or false, then this implies a transcendent of *some* kind, a structure in which no further possible piece of information could logically reverse the rightness or truth of the perceived piece of information. This transcendent could be God, or some manifestation of God, and hence take an overtly religious form, but it need not. All that can be established is that a self-consistent scientific empiricism must do without certainty. Perhaps empiricism can do without certainty (as in consistent forms of Bayesian epistemology), but the development of such an empiricism has proved awkward, and is often preempted by confused foundations. Empiricism tends toward a foundational form based on the certainty of some form of sense perception, just the move that entails some form of transcendence on Kolakowski's account.

The perceived separation of science and religion allows a scientific study of religion resulting in an anthropology of religion, a sociology of religion, a comparative religion, and even an economics of religion. In a general way, the presupposition of separation combined with a scientific epistemology results in a picture of religion which is largely determined by this starting point. Scientific study of religion is restricted to the natural trappings of current religion, institutional membership and expressed belief being the outstanding purchase points for the application of scientific method. All religions, presented simultaneously as the object of comparative religion, force a conception of relativism or of the unimportance and superficiality of the investigations, even though the results might be interesting. Comparative religion becomes similar to comparative plumbing, or comparative cookery, and can only answer the same sorts of distributional questions. To understand any of these things in any depth, complex relationships between history, climate, available resources, and so on, must be carefully studied, a task defying anything but years of concentrated local assimilation of an alien culture. A single anthropologist cannot be expected to internalize very many cultures in this way. Further, other major religious systems, like Christianity, take on so many variants that generalization is extremely hazardous, especially generalization from externally observed statistics. We are interested in other cultures, and other religions, of course, and it is not wrong to develop this interest, particularly as it can throw incidental light on our own problems and their possible solution. What is under discussion is whether a scientific study of various religions can produce insight and explanation rather than anecdotal information about the forms of religiosity in other settings. Consider the variety of personal expression of religion within any major Christian church, and multiply it by the range of alternative major religions, and the magnitude of the problem is obvious. Must there be, in some straightforward sense, scientific knowledge about such material?

Within anthropology and sociology, religion has been frequently studied in the context of functionalism. Religion normally provides a sacred origin for the society in mythical terms and presents an institution whose rituals are (relatively) invariant over time, thus contributing functionally to the stability of society. But functionalism has a tendency to ignore the contradictory aspects of human life in favor of a view that consistent facts and a consistent analysis of societal structure can be read from the surface of nature. The values expressed in survey data, for example, may not be irrelevant to microlevel action, but may be related to specific actions in contradictory ways mediated through the unconscious.[17] Beliefs are often clustered as a consequence in unexpected ways. Plain dress and dominant religious concerns may be linked with positive or negative attitudes toward technological progress, as the Shakers and the Amish illustrate.[18] The linkage is not logical so much as it is psychological or social, and when these dimensions are filtered out by queries about belief, the linkage is apt to seem arbitrary. People often act on the basis of belief systems that they cannot control in the sense that they cannot articulate them in a coherent deductive structure, something that seems true of nearly all religiously motivated behavior. As one descends from elite theoretical groups attached to some movement, the grasp of the theoretical principles of that movement are likely to be lost, and to be replaced by clusters of concrete issues between which only a historical, psychological, or social link can be found, if any. At the elite level, members of a movement may be able to articulate consistent theoretical structure, but be open as to their precise identity within the movement, whereas at a lower level, identity in the movement as expressed by a concrete issue will be obvious in the absence of the ability to articulate theoretical structure. The elite of a religious organization may be willing to discuss change in theoretical structure in intellectual abstraction whereas lower-level involvement may be geared to an identity expressed in terms of a concrete commitment.[19] Consequently, the same problem of complexity that engenders pressure toward trivial results infects the study of a fixed complex institution as much as it infects more abstract attempts to pursue comparative religion.

There have recently been attempts to study religion through economic models; for example, models derived from human capital theory.[20] Such attempts may look at time allocation or money allocation to religious institutions, as a function of such variables as income level or rate of income increase over time. Curiously, to make such studies interesting, time and money allotment to religion are seen as an investment toward consumption in an afterlife. A woman's much lower available market wages may free her for time allotments to religion, and the feeling that the probability of dying is increasing may place greater pressure on all older wage earners to invest time or money in religion, a money investment in a church institution being more rational than a time investment (in the economic sense) for higher-income workers. This line of thinking can explain the higher rate of female time allotments and the increasing time allotments of human beings, at least into middle age, that are observed, for example, in the United States. Economic models, which recognize an afterlife as a motivating belief but can give it no ontological status, a curious wrinkle in a scientific approach, also show the familiar tendency to represent religion in terms of institutions and official systems of belief.

It is perhaps worth attempting an assessment of the general conclusions that come from the scientific study of religion. As societies are studied along a spectrum from the primitive societies of ethnographic writing to modern technological societies, a gradual separation of science and religion and associated institutions becomes obvious. Religion tends to become associated with participation in religious institutional life or acceptance of the belief patterns associated with such institutions. What is then seen is a great shift toward secularization. Religion occupies a smaller percentage of life, that is, there is a smaller period of time in which one is primarily engaged in religious study or activity. A rather large and possibly increasing segment of society has very little association with religious institutions, and may seem totally secular. There are associated phenomena. Our use of language becomes more divided, so that the language of science and the language of religion become different, and each codes the status of its domain. When the standard of scientific syntax is laid against primitive language, primitive language and primitive thought appear symbolic, i.e., not to be scientific and literal. In fact, the data indicate change, but they do not indicate more than that unless further assumptions are made, consciously or nonconsciously. Secularization has occurred only if religion is located solely in religious institutions, and the absence of the symbolic in modern scientific language may be nothing other than seeing modern religious language as similar to primitive language, because it is manifestly dissimilar in many respects to modern scientific language. The assumptions made in such secularization arguments are obviously questionable. We shall proceed on the basis that *change* has occurred, but that by itself change is a trivial concomitant of chronological time. We shall attempt to see whether religion hasn't shifted its location from traditional religious institutions, at least partially, and whether the legacy of primitive symbolism isn't shared among sacred and secular discourses, rather than being compressed totally into overtly religious language. In other words, we shall pursue the idea that secularization is an artifact of an unexamined assumption about the location of religious belief.

The use of modern science as the legitimate epistemological access to nature often results in downgrading magic and religion to the status of imperfect attempts to achieve science, that is, imperfect attempts to understand and control nature. The primitive just seems to have had incorrect beliefs, partly because of the absence of science in primitive society. Primitives may have seen the world as more widely populated by human or animate agencies whose operations could be influenced by communication through ritual, but primitive skepticism is also not unknown. Although there are plenty of primitive societies that have either disappeared or changed dramatically through interaction with modern technological societies, there is reason to believe that their methods of interacting with their world were often quite rational given their situations, situations not to be confused with their stage of development as we perceive it with the instrumentality of science in hand. Primitives are hardly to be faulted for not having bent their energies to developing science, instead of continuing traditional ways, for where would the conception of science and the relevant practices have come from? It is partly a mystery why so many primitive religions should have cooperated in behavior that from our perspective can be seen as entailing rational breeding and survival strategies, but the fact is undeniable, and it indicates that the sheer charge of primitivism is irrelevant.

Let us consider witchcraft in this connection. Certain forms of witchcraft arise in many small societies with well-defined borders, sometimes defined partly by isolation.[21] Such societies may be organized around the decisions of a single leader, and the obedience of other societal members to that leader, a social structure that is obviously limited in its potential size. A social structure of this kind that has grown to the limits, or close to the limits, of its potential for control may be served by fission, so that the structure can be reproduced in two new groups. The emergence of a new leader, and allegiance to him, cannot occur within the confines and demands of the old structure, which demand allegiance to the single leader. Witchcraft accusations between the old and emerging leader, however, disassociate the normal structure, allowing a period of time in which fission can occur without violation of the normal rules of propriety. From our point of view, the witch can have no "occult" powers. In fact, the powers of the witch could be felt only inside the relevant society, where the relationship between the old leader and the new leader give the latter "powers" that cannot be fully articulated until the new social structure exists. Witchcraft powers can thus function rationally in permitting separation and regrouping of a society whose structure is bound by this traditional form. Our social structure is different, and displays different nodes where social relations can produce positional powers that are not easily articulated. Insofar as religion is related to a given social structure, it may deal with positional powers that can only be understood by participants in that structure. A great deal of what seems misguided in earlier cultures may be related to this fact, and the fact that not very many detailed purely instrumental and scientific problems may be common to the past and our situation, making comparisons cloudy. We shall proceed on the assumption that religions, in spite of universalistic claims that may be part of an attempt to increase cultural influence, are, in fact, products of specific cultural and historical situations, and are rational only insofar as they address principal problems felt by individuals in those situations.

We have examined the current situation of separation of domain between science and religion, and the impact on the perceived nature of religion due to this separation. Assumptions about the epistemological privilege of science seem to have inevitably biased the standpoint from which religion has been studied, inevitably forcing a view of modernity as entailing increasing secularization. Religion has been located in institutional structure and belief systems, and a study of this location confirms the general diagnosis of irrelevance and stagnation.

Contemporary philosophy of science suggests that what one can observe depends on what one thinks it theoretically possible to observe. We will make some new assumptions based on this perspective. The first is that the institutional structures and belief systems of Christianity have largely developed in the past, and were rational responses to past historical situations.[22] Perhaps religion in our time is partially or wholly located elsewhere than in the institutional belief systems of Christianity, and the whole direction of scientific attention has been mislocated. We will be primarily interested in a better understanding of our religious situation, that is, the religious situation in the United States in the 1980s. On sound hermeneutical grounds, we will start with our prejudices and pre-understandings, studying other major contemporary religious situations only in an attempt to understand our own better, without any presumption that other situations can be coherently grasped through a mere study of texts. We shall not assume that a religion need make reference to divinities, to particular rituals or myths, or that it need have an *articulated* system of belief. Rather, we shall take a religion to be a picture of how the world ought to be, expressed at least partially as a set of values that seem imposed on us, rather than as a set of values that we are free to choose. These values will be seen as spiritual, otherworldly, or nonmaterial, and they will indicate how one should conduct oneself in the natural or secular world. Assumption of a religion may lead to conflict with other values, particularly with those adopted by people not sharing one's religion. Most important, religion can thus provide a point of critique for the way in which others live their lives, and even the way one is living one's own life, while providing a justification for the way one would like to live one's own life, or thinks that one should live one's own life. These opinions obviously will extend to a criticism of surrounding society.

The closest secular experience to religious conversion may be the result of travel. Staying in a foreign country long enough to permit integration of what at first seems incomprehensibly different ways of doing things may result in a new perspective when one returns home.[23] Perhaps one's university seems different and some of the old "natural" ways no longer seem so obviously correct—or they may seem even more correct. The world is different in the sense that one reacts to it differently, judges it differently, but the measurable aspects of the world may be the same. Buildings have the same size and relationship, and are filled with the same number of people. It is hard to describe the experience to others, but it is real enough, and there is no reason to be bullied out of it simply because a measurable change cannot be located.

Religion has sometimes been presented as the highest values held by a person or a society. If this is coupled with the idea that certain features of human life, death, and the threat of violence, for example, are universal, it might seem that the distinctive features of religion could be determined by abstracting from lower-level values to whatever might be agreed on by all human beings. Further, the origins of religion may lie in the accommodation of death, or the desire to prevent social disintegration through violence, but this constancy can't begin to explain the observed *variety* of world religions.[24] Relativism and error might, but it is just as possible that the variety is due to specific relationships to the historical societies of origin and continuance of the religions, which may add features of religion not to be accounted for by common themes or irrationality. In other words, the main thread of religion may be one of potential opposition or criticism of a surrounding society by development of a picture of life as how it should be lived. The opposition may or may not be apparent, depending on the nature of the surrounding society. What is being suggested is that the core of religion is potentially critical rather than functional or accommodating. Religious people may prefer to destroy or leave a sufficiently repugnant surrounding society, rather than accommodate to it, where the motivating force of opposition comes from the religious conception of a life in order. Many of the major religions have begun with such opposition, or have been sustained by prophets drawing on the strength of some religious conception of a correct life. The Judaic and Christian traditions seem particularly involved with such oppositional possibilities, as in the case of the Old Testament prophets, and a large part of our later observations are concerned to indicate that the possibility of critical distance on surrounding society is the part of religious heritage most important in our time, and most obscured by the accommodation of professional denominationalism to overtly secular forces.[25]

It is perhaps the fact that religion and science are separated in our conceptual framework that allows us to look back and partially set aside the functional picture of religion as a stabilizing institution within society.[26] Of course, what we see as secular and sacred are mixed up in earlier societies, and many societal offices combined secular and sacred roles. Religion did not transcend natural experience under these circumstances, but its critical distance is not absent. A king, for example, may combine secular and sacred functions, but historically is rarely the author of the sacred, as opposed to a mediator of the sacred. Sacred criticism thus remains a possible check on a king's secular authority, even if the criticism has to be articulated by members of a priesthood partially fearful for their lives. Ritual festivals also provided space in which the normal secular order could be criticized, and, in some cases, space in which the king could even be deposed or killed. Critique of the king would hardly have emanated from the royal presence. And in a successful society, there would be no necessity for articulated sacred criticism. Functionalism has overemphasized stability, and overlooked the fact that society can be strengthened through religious renewal as a result of sacred critique.

The possibility of critique helps to explain the curious partial overlap of morality and religion in history. Some mores of concern to religious values will have sacred sanction, but others will be largely independent of such sanction. It follows that some things that a person ought to do are matters of secular convenience or co-ordination, where the obligation has force, but is ultimately conventional in some sense. On the other hand, some things that a person ought to do threaten pollution or disaster if ignored, and will have sharply circumscribed obligations in performance. Some of these obligations will be concerned with one's relationship to the sacred, and not overtly to one's fellow human beings, so the two domains are not everywhere congruent.

We can now turn to the problem of defining religion for our purposes. As our discussion has already indicated, we are assuming that religion is represented in any society by a set of values that seems imposed or imperative rather than just a matter of choice.[27] Such values may or may not be articulated in the society, and they may be difficult to locate or notice. Most of the rest of this investigation will be concerned with developing this notion to determine whether or not such values can be located in the contemporary world. We are trying not to prejudge secularization; it may turn out that contemporary human beings are as religious as any humans have ever been, or that they participate in more than one religion in a somewhat novel pattern. Our investigation will be philosophical rather than sociological or scientific. Systems of belief will not be examined nor will institutional membership be crucial. Although we must look at the major religions, an obvious place to begin, we will not suppose that the denominational churches need be other than historical relics. As for belief, it is clear that beliefs are not central to many religions historically, and that religion need not be a separable component of culture.[28] We will look for values, and then determine how they may be related to articulated belief systems or recognizable components of our culture. Some religions are based on appropriate action, or mythic variation on central themes, and we cannot suppose that articulation of religion by acceptance of belief statements has to be a feature of contemporary religiosity.[29]

We will be looking only at the contemporary situation in the United States. Christianity will be important for our investigation, but will not exhaust it, and our investigation is not motivated by a desire to defend Christianity. This major religion has major variations in France, Germany, Sweden, England, Latin America, and the United States. In the United States, however, it does not regularly confront older folk religions that it must accommodate. It cannot be assumed that anything valid discovered here can be generalized to other contemporary situations. We have adumbrated the claim that the religious tradition retains positions that can be developed into critique of surrounding society. Because of this, it may turn out that an accommodated Christianity may have the weakest potential for critique of American society, whereas an unaccommodated Marxism or Judaism may have strong potential for critique. The situation may be precisely reversed, for example, in Eastern European countries. But as we shall see, the visions involved in critique in the two places may be more coincident than official theologies could permit, a curious fact, but one not in conflict with what has already been said if the societies to be criticized are sufficiently similar at this point in history. Perhaps this is sufficient to indicate the fascinating potentialities of the following line of investigation. We now need to turn to the question of how imposed values can be discerned in contemporary society.

2

Major Contemporary Theologies

CHAPTER ANALYSIS In this chapter, I will begin the development of religion as critique by looking at six contemporary major religious traditions in terms of their theological resources. These six religions, including Christianity, are grouped into two sets of theologies according to some basic historical differences in outlook. At the theological level, these religious traditions seem to advance quite divergent beliefs and attitudes at a very high level of abstraction. As only the potential for social critique is of central interest to us, the epistemological status of these systems is not of any particular relevance to our project. If religions were simply belief systems, as noted in the last chapter, then incompatibilities between these traditions would require that we make comparative epistemological judgments, with the result that, at most, one of these systems could be evaluated as true. We are not in any way attempting here what is usually regarded as comparative religion. The sole purpose of this survey is to consider the conceptual and pictorial resources of these traditions as they are relevant to generating social critique. It is a reminder of facts that will be utilized in later discussion. Ultimately, of course, we are primarily interested in the current potential of Christianity as a source of social critique, but the possibilities for Christian critique are most coherently surveyed against a realization of the protean adaptability of religious traditions in general.

In the next chapter we will see how these divergent resources can be utilized to find convergent forms of specific critique associated with the different theological metaphors when these are brought to bear on similar, specific social problems.

In an effort to come to terms with the significance of contemporary Christianity, we shall begin by comparing some general features of Christian theology to general features of other major contemporary religious systems. The systems used here as foils to Christianity are Judaism, Islam, Marxism, Hinduism, and Buddhism. Selecting these six systems for comparative remarks is based on their survival value in the contemporary world as well as on their relationship to Christianity. Thus we are ignoring the kaleidoscope of contemporary religions accepted by smaller numbers of adherents, and, to some extent, ignoring larger Chinese and Japanese complexes. Six systems seem to suffice for the purposes at hand, since the five foils to Christianity have some form of major representation and encounter with Christianity in the United States. Survival, of course, has been seen by all the major religions as a possible sign of their truth, since in many cases these religions have arisen from a crucible in which similar alternative religions have now disappeared. No attempt can be made here to consider possible reasons for the success of these religions, but their longevity and success will have the effect of demanding autonomous treatment.

Our six systems can be conveniently gathered into two historically connected groups; one group consists of Judaism, Christian-

ity, Islam, and Marxism, and the other consists of Hinduism and
Buddhism. In each group, an indigenous set of religious insights has
been modified and reformed by later religious development. Christianity was originally a splinter of Judaism, and Islam in turn has
incorporated much of Judaism and Christianity. Christianity often
views Judaism as a partial revelation of God, and similarly Islam
often views Judaism and Christianity as partial revelations of God
leading to the fuller revelation of the Prophet. Marxism, consciously atheistic, arises in a Christian setting which obviously colors the
structure of Marxist belief. Buddhism, on the other hand, can be
viewed as a reform movement originally appearing with Hinduism.
Other reform movements of Hinduism (Sikhism, Jainism) as well as
other developments from Judaism (Greek Orthodoxy, Babism,
Bahai) will be ignored here. Our basic structure is that of two
seminal religious explosions that have subsequently been adapted
into other, divergent major religions.

At the root of these two traditions are two quite divergent sets of
ideas, although the subsequent forms of adaptation may appear to
make historical branches overlap, even some that arise within the
separate traditions. The Judaic legacy depends on taking the natural world as a serious arena, if only as a place where an important
drama preparatory to life in another, more permanent world, occurs. Agency, the connection between individual action and its outcome, the existence of individuals having a single lifetime in the
natural world, are all essential aspects of this insight. Time and
space also play a central role in defining this world, and the notion
of agency within it. All the religions in this grouping have a canon
of sacred texts representing the legitimated words of the founder or
of God's legitimated revelation to a founder for his followers. The
modern features of these variants, authoritative answers to significant questions traceable to text, and the importance of the natural
world, are clearly compatible with the features of modern science
as it has developed in the West. The other tradition downplays
individual agency as well as the significance of the natural world,
and has a much more complex attitude toward sacred text and the
expectation of fixed abstract answers for religious questions. Al-

though such grand themes divide the two traditions, it is possible to find converging similarities between some of the variants. Marxism and Buddhism, for example, tend not to trace responsiblity for man's place in the universe to divine origins, and suppose that improvement in the human condition must come from correct human action, rather than from divine intervention. This fact points to some considerable difficulties in attempting to effect a clean conceptual separation of the traditions.

Further difficulties arise because all the religious systems have conservative and progressive strains, as well as inner and outer oriented strains. The first division is roughly between strains that attempt to preserve purity as it is discerned in the original form of the religion, and those that attempt to develop a form of the religion of direct relevance to modern life. Progressive strains, for example, may permit modified satisfaction of ritual demands to accommodate air flight, or business transactions with foreign corporations. Inner and outer strains will be oriented toward correct consciousness or correct forms of ritual performance as the defining characteristic of orthodoxy, most larger church denominations attempting a compromise between these orientations. All the traditions will consequently show a variety of institutional forms which arise from the pressure toward division which these tendencies, and others, engender. And then, of course, individuals and social groups will find different ways of accommodating institutional demands in their own lives, a matter of considerable complexity across social classes and between different cultural areas where a religion is practiced.[1] In what follows, differences will be observed between positions that are in some sense intuitively central and differentiating with respect to these traditions; otherwise, the complexity of variant forms would swamp any attempt to reach the kind of analysis we are after.

As has often been observed, the modern Christian tradition is an amalgam of Judaic religious intuitions with Greek logic and philosophy. Christianity, as well as the other major religions, has no doubt had to shift positions as a result of dialogue and confrontation with other major religions. Modern Judaic discussions of

God's nature, for example, show the impact of both Christian theology and modern philosophy on the questions and answers considered appropriate. The fecundity of the Western intellectual
tradition may well be due largely to the complex variants in the
interplay of Greek and Judaic ideas, which are not natural allies. To
look effectively at the founding Judaic ideas in the first religious
tradition, we need to return imaginatively to the pre-Christian position. Pastoralism lies at the root of pre-Christian Judaism. The
pastoralist lives in a place of clear delineations, day and night, val-
ley and wilderness, and interacts with an orderly universe in the
large, as displayed, for example, in the night sky and weather patterns, but with a disorderly and changing universe at the local level,
particularly as he or she moves or changes location. Landscape
must be observed with a disinterested eye for clues to action, and it
is not primarily a haunt of spirits, or a location for aesthetic enjoyment. Intensity of interaction with nature may preclude disinterested contemplation of it, except for the long-term aspects, such as
the sky. The sky is settled and orderly; what is in the sand is constantly changing.[2] God may show his presence in rainbows,
thunder, or pestilence, as well as indirectly in local nature, which is
alive, formed by God, but not subject to universal law, rather to
God's personality. Differences with a Greek view are implicit in
such observations, as the relatively static Greek intellectual could
invest time in the contemplative study of nature's changes, even at
the local level. Major differences are related to the action potential
of Judaic culture, a potential focused on dynamism and change,
and on the significance of one's group as a hedge against the future
in an uncertain and potentially devastating local environment.
There is, in ancient Judaic literature, no description of the appearance of things, but instead descriptions of how to build and do
things, and fixed rules for personal conduct.[3] Long periods of waiting seem to have produced deep and abstract thought about God,
an omniscient, somewhat arbitrary creature, who created man in
his image, which clearly means with similar powers rather than
with an externally similar appearance. Pastoralists are homocen-
tric, patriarchal, and dualistic, with a religion turned away from

immanence in the natural environment. The God of the Jews was a God of nomads, attached to *them*, and not to the place where they happened to be. This God sacralized laws and ethics within that group, which was a means of preserving identity of the group with change in place, or even during dispersion. A monotheistic God can demand the same moral standards for all, particularly for all people in the group he reveals himself to, and tends to convey a morality along with a religious code. The Judaic demand for social justice and acceptance of community suffering, the later Christian concept of every life to be lived in Christ's image, and the Muslim notions of obedience and almsgiving, all show an implied group boundary partially defined by a revelation within which a uniform code of conduct could be expected of every human being.

The religious genius of Judaism, however, is to be found centrally located in the conception of the Covenant between God and his chosen people. No matter how unique this may have been, its brilliance is indisputable. Wherever God may have been located in other cultures in an icon, the capture of the icon and its destruction had to spell trouble for the reputation of the god. The Jewish God never appears as an object in the world, but is totally apart from his creation. A covenantal relationship was conceived of as a set of two-way promises, the Jews promising to live as God's chosen people, as an example justifying God's revelation to them, in exchange for which God promised to protect them. Defeats could no longer be a sign of God's weakness, since a defeat for the Jews could be read as a warning, under the Covenant, that the sins of Jewish citizens were provoking God into anger, an anger that might result in warning or punishment. This covenantal relationship is a personal one, and not one of a scientific generalization to possibly falsifying instances. The obvious consequence of God's existence is that his relationship is based on communication and understanding and reciprocal trust, and his existence is not made a matter of counterexample based on instances. God's existence is taken as a fact; but his relationship to his creation can vary over time depending on what happens in the creation. The covenantal relationship is indisputably sheer religious genius; it keeps a culture potentially alive and viable in almost any circumstances. It depends on a model of constant personal relationship rather than on an epistemological function. God's variable relationship under the Covenant to his followers allows not only criticism of other cultures, but criticism of a culture in which Jews live even when they are subjected to persecution within it, and it may be this feature that is essential in creating the critical potential of the first of the two major traditions that we have singled out for consideration.

Graven images of God were forbidden in the covenantal relationship. Viewed instrumentally, this avoids the localization of God and God's possible embarrassment if the image is attacked; this also serves as a reminder that God is not *in* the world.[4] But this bears an interesting relationship to a second major feature of the Judaic foundations of interest to us. Man is said to be made in God's image. Now in other cultures, for example Greek culture, the gods were taken to be so much like human beings that they could appear on earth and interact with human beings without necessarily being recognized as gods. The image of God in Judaism, on the other hand, is the start of God's transcendence essential to the religious tradition dependent on Judaic foundations. Man does not look like God in the sense that human beings share God's sensual form or appearance, rather man possesses speech, language, and thought, and hence can act like God while being part of the natural world.[5] God can speak with man, permitting the possibility of the covenantal relationship, while remaining totally distinct from man in appearance. Man now transcends the rest of creation, as God transcends man. Further, God has no natural origin, does not come from a creature like natural creatures as he does in some other creation myths, but is a transcendent force that can breathe life into man who thus also transcends natural creatures, and can deal with them through the use of names and language. God, in himself, cannot be known, or understood merely through his name, but only as he presents himself to human beings.

Some of Jewish history presents a dialectical tension between a tendency toward representation and the manifest drive toward nonrepresentation. The worship of the calf and the construction of

the Tabernacle, on the one hand, are opposed to strict interpretations of God's prohibition on representation. God, of course, was
not to be seen as appearance in either location, being represented as
fecund in the one case, and as capable of being heard in the other.
Original services may have involved animal sacrifice, in common
with other religions, where a scapegoat could be instrumental in
renewing the covenant. But the function of the covenant over time
was to permit the gradual dominance of nonrepresentative forms as
a result of historical experience. The exile, the destruction of the
Temple, the Diaspora, were not to be interpreted as God's desertion of the Jews, but as their desertion of God through failure to
keep their covenantal requirements. Gradually the transcendence
from location became a fixed part of the legacy to later religions,
and an instrumental part in their longevity.[6] The use of language
became a sign of the historical situation. God's language as originally revealing the names of things in his creation was in mythic
history split into languages no longer mirroring nature, and the
language of the world, especially the profane languages of the non-
Jews, have broken with the original covenantal relationship. Redemption must be coded into the recovery of a universal, comprehensive language.[7]

There were no social class distinctions according to the original
covenantal relationship, nor was man lifted clearly to a position of
dominance over nature. Every person was to be holy; to keep the
Covenant. This is the reverse significance of the fact that there is no
priesthood in the Rabbinical tradition, and of the fact that no man
(including especially Moses) becomes God in orthodox Judaism.
Slaves, further, are seen as human beings, capable of attaining
freedom.[8] Animals must be treated with consideration as part of
the total creation. The state is a later conception, arising at the time
of David and the subsequent kings, but this expresses the fact that
the covenantal relationship is prior to the relationships of state, and
can form the basis of critique of the state, especially a corrupt state.
The kings, as is clear from history, often acted in a manner that
called forth condemnation from righteous citizens. This is the basis
for religious opposition within Judaic society, and, of course, the

basis for Jewish religious opposition within any society where Jews may form a minority class. Unassimilated and outsider status has been common for Jews during their history, and they have frequently been predominant in articulate, critical social subgroups to the present time.

Christianity begins as a form of Judaism, as can be seen by the fact that Jesus seems primarily bent on reforms within the Jewish community of his time. He lives in it, mostly in rural areas, and he addresses theoretical questions raised by the Sadducees and Pharisees.[9] All general remarks about Judaism will apply as a consequence to at least some historical Christians, but Christian doctrine becomes distinct from Judaic theology as Christian theology develops. First, Christianity depends on the idea that Jesus was himself God (the son of God) and part of the Trinity. Jesus' divinity is incompatible with the major thrust of orthodox Judaic theology, which cannot recognize the idea of God's appearing in this way on earth. The miracles of Jesus were taken by early Christians to establish his divinity, and were decisive in arguing for the truth of Christianity. Whether God actually spoke to Moses or merely inspired Moses to write down the Law can be squared with different versions of Judaic theology. But there is no potential ambiguity in the life of Jesus. If he didn't actually turn water into wine, or feed thousands on a few fish and some loaves, the stories of miracles in the New Testament are just hoaxes, and undercut the religious authority of that document for modern readers. The crucial miracle among all of them, of course, is the Resurrection. Either Jesus did or did not arise from the dead. The early Christian had to accept such miracles right from the start, and, once this was done, other relative minutiae of credal belief about his or her faith could hardly prove differentially embarrassing.[10] Christ's status as a theologian is given by his teachings, which seem immanent to Judaic issues of theology. The irrational flavor of Christianity may have ironically made later Greek conversion more, rather than less, likely. If Christianity had had to depend on logic or the philosophical superiority of its moral code, it might have been lost in argument with other religions, and if it had had to depend initially on force, it was without a power base. Conversion to what is seen as irrational in the contemporary worldview may prove a powerful stimulus toward conversion, especially when the desire to criticize contemporary society takes a dominant place in motivation.

Miracles, of course, are to be found outside the Christian tradition. There are miracles in Jewish tradition, such as the parting of the Red Sea, but they are interpreted as God's acting in the world, and not as miracles performed in the world by divine actors resembling human shape. The former idea causes no problems given the historical nature of God. The miracles in Eastern religions usually show the power of mind over matter, or the immateriality of the world, rather than the divinity of the miracle worker. Other miracle workers contemporary with Jesus were frequently taken to be God, or to be divine, by their followers, but such claims usually lost impact after the death of the "God" in question. Jesus Christ, as God's son, could be resurrected after death due to the undiminished powers of God the Father. The theological brilliance of this is really lost completely if Jesus is made merely a prophet or a wise man, as he is in many modern versions of Christianity, since his sayings or remarks by themselves (apart from references to his divine status) have no corner on wisdom in the context of other interpreters of the Judaic tradition.

The doctrine of the Trinity is quite nicely conflated with Christianity's claim to being a universal religion. Christianity is not tied to the notion of a chosen people; it is rather that those who have received the revelation of God through the historical Jesus are obligated to spread this good news to others no matter what their social position. Of course, many countries, areas, and so forth, were converted to Christianity, often in ways permitting Christianity's adaptation to the local religion. In this process of adaptation to existent local forms, the Trinity has proved a brilliant tactical device. If the Trinity is emphasized, Christianity can be displayed in a polytheistic form, and prove adaptable to polytheistic sensibilities. Because of this, some historians in other cultural traditions have described Christianity as a polytheistic interlude between the more austere monotheisms of Judaism and Islam. If the Trinity is not emphasized, Christianity is clearly a monotheism. This possibility for doctrinal variety can still be seen within Christianity. Nothing of the Catholic doctrine about Mary, for example, appears in many forms of Protestantism, although both Protestantism and Catholicism trace their doctrines to biblical texts, and it is clear that this flexibility of Christian interpretation can prove extremely accommodating in the conversion process.

After Christianity's earthly success, and during its development in the Roman Empire, many of its originally absurd beliefs (perhaps deliberately absurd) were tamed in an encounter with Greek philosophy and its dichotomies. Many possible interpretations of such doctrines as the Incarnation and the Trinity were developed until orthodox sets of beliefs could be established which were rationally defensible in scholarly dispute. An extremely imporant part of this process was an intensification of the relative transcendence of mankind. God becomes more transcendent in Christianity than he had been in Judaism, but people become raised also over and against nature, able to dominate it for their own ends because of an alienated relationship emphasizing the immortal soul of humans as a characteristic making them sharply distinct from nature. The relationship of people to God becomes reasoned and cerebral. Christianity's God did not interact emotionally or arbitrarily in people's lives, and God could neither envy nor ridicule human beings, and did not punish them (necessarily) during earthly life.[11] Earthly life, in theory, becomes less important for religious purposes, in that proper belief could insure salvation somewhat independently of actual human action. An inner state becomes the criterion of acceptability, and envy between human beings is downgraded to a lamentable human failing on earth. The signs of this increasingly transcendental progress are mixed, and require evaluation. God becomes less humanlike, a rational calculating agent who understands the universe we live in because he created it.[12] God acquires powers, omniscience, omnipotence, for example, that can be sharply separated philosophically from properties of human beings. On the other hand, Jesus, or even God himself, may be pictured, which seems to tell against transcendence. It may well be the case that the obvious and established transcendence of God in Christianity allows Jesus to be pictured because that cannot threaten confusion or anthropomorphism under these circumstances. Indeed, Jesus is not thought to be in God's form, so the fact that only he appears as a human being indicates subtly that God the Father is quite different. This is not changed by representations of God over angelic hosts which stand between him and humans. And, of course, only the persons of the Trinity could be pictured, not the Trinity itself, preserving its mystery. Further, the transcendence of God may call for an intermediary with more human features to establish a link between human beings and God. Unlike religions where fate is stressed, God must be accessible in some form for counsel to imperfect human beings. In Neoplatonic conceptions, as well as in Catholicism, a vast chain of intermediary creatures (e.g., angels) stands in to mediate between human beings and God. The connection is remote enough that only the Church, through elaborate ceremony, is able to interpret correctly divine ordinance. Protestantism reestablishes direct contact between believer and God, but does this at the expense of God's rationality, making him a force too powerful and mysterious to be completely rationally comprehended. Calvin, for example, saw man as alienated from his fellowman (becoming literally asocial) *and* as alienated from God by the Fall.[13] Transcendence is maintained by making God less intelligible, even if he can speak directly to men without the intervention of the Church.

The Christian doctrine of original sin can be seen as reinforcing increasing transcendence. Other major religions see human beings as innately good, or at least as potentially good. But God can't share sin with human beings. Original sin also plays down the significance of pleasure and reward in this life, thus increasing the contrast with the afterlife, and the transcendent qualities of life after death. Modern churches that have accommodated surrounding society in an effort to attain a suitable secular status must downplay this notion, and considerably weaken the dire prognostications for the possibilities of attaining heaven that are associated with the original doctrine.

Greek philosophy and Christianity produced an amalgam of
ideas in which religious positions were determined by deduction
from texts, by tracing out their presumed intellectual consequences. The result is exclusivity between sects, and ultimately the
problem of hermeneutical translation of texts. In other religious
traditions, for example, belief can be a private matter in the sense
that publicly correct behavior can be legitimately coupled with
individual exploration of religious belief that seems appropriate to
one's station in life. Christianity has seen fit to penetrate this inwardness, and to insist on a unique reading of biblical text as
a criterion for correct faith within its various branches.[14] But this
view won out only gradually and reached full flower with Protestantism; it was originally mingled with a view of texts that is more
common elsewhere. A text may contain various readings simultaneously, some more esoteric than others, just as a human being
may say several things at once in making a particular utterance.
Hermeneutical traditions can be devoted to locating the simultane-
ity of meanings on various levels that a text may present. But where
many meanings are thought simultaneously present, correct interpretation becomes more a matter of allowing all the meanings to
influence the course of one's life, without necessarily apportioning
the strength of the meanings according to one precise, orthodox
function. Other religions show doctrinal splits and factionaliza-
tion, to be sure, but Christianity is preeminent with its insistence
that correct belief systems displayed in a consistent philosophical
organization should be the defining feature of religious differences.

Before leaving Christianity, we might note one aspect of its
teachings of considerable import for later consideration of its social
aspects. Whereas Judaism historically has been the religion of a
small, relatively weak state, or the religion of a minority within
some larger society, Christianity has been the official religion of
many large and powerful states. There has been hierarchy inside
Christian churches and in Christian societies, as well as class
conflict. Further, many Christian churches have memberships that
belong predominantly to a narrow socioeconomic stratum. But
Christianity *theoretically* preaches the same message to all human

beings, regardless of class or social position. The Hellenic religions did not do this, and neither do most Eastern religions. This feature permits Christianity to present a picture of life on earth as ideally lived in societies of equality, as well as picturing life in heaven as lived in a society of equality. This vision makes contact with social visions in Judaism and Marxism, quite independently of other theological differences between versions of the three.

When we turn to Islam, to some extent the imaginary line between West and East is crossed, and interpretation becomes more problematic. There is no doubt that what is Eastern or oriental is defined as a mysterious negativity in opposition to Western self-conceptions, and this psychologically constructed East is then instantiated in experience much as theory influences observation elsewhere.[15] Islamic culture is clearly more totalistic than our own, making less marked contrasts between church and state, or between religion and everyday life. This is marked by the religious demand for alms for the sick, poor, and widowed in the surrounding society. Resistance or struggle is often religious and political, in some sense, with political opposition capable of being expressed through religious observations. If the religious aspect is discussed or noticed, rather than the political, it has the effect of making the opposition appear irrational in our terms, since it appears based on (irrational) religious beliefs that are not instrumental in our culture for attaining political ends. Differences in the contemporary treatment of Israel and Iran, for example, and in our mere perception of them, are at least partly traceable to the arbitrariness involved in such labeling as it impinges on our conception of separation of spheres of influence.[16] Islam may be a vital component in attempting political independence from larger national entities because national self-identity requires a partly religious, or inherently religious, expression.

To a certain extent, Islam can be viewed as a marriage of Judaic ideas with sustained earthly power.[17] Muhammad, like Moses, found revelation through migration, but Islamic civilization didn't have to come up from below (like Christianity), or deal with such severe earthly defeats as the Babylonian Exile or the destruction of the Temple. Both religions, Islam and Judaism, are patriarchal monotheisms that forbid direct representation of divinity. Sustained power on earth from the beginning, however, characterizes Islamic history, and explains why church and state should be so firmly welded conceptually. There is a natural link between Islamic thought and nationalism. By contrast, for example, Calvinism had to reach back to Judaic roots without an intervening legitimate concept of the state, or at least without a very rich intervening concept. Christianity presents a religion of another world, a spiritual polity, and can be purely oppositional to any state within which it is located. In Europe, the fact that the Greek and Christian origins were distinct, and never completely amalgamated, allowed science to develop for those who were interested in reading the book of nature. Muslim thought seems inherently more mystical regarding the universe, although it permits satisfaction in earthly pleasure. Perhaps the mysticism was crucial to the development of mathematics in Muslim culture, without which modern European science would seem not to have been possible. In any event, Islam has only one origin, the original religious state of Muhammad. For intellectual stimulus, Europeans can turn back to the opposition between Greek views and Christianity, and to later confrontations such as those occurring in the Reformation, Renaissance, and even to local political movements of independence. It is not easy to understand Islamic culture from a similar perspective, because the clash of opposing views does not play the same prominent role in Islamic history.

Islam is comfortable with power and happiness on this earth, in spite of formal resemblances to Western monotheism, including a doctrine of the afterlife. Muslims can be comfortable in their family settings without worrying about the future or seeking redemption. The doctrine of original sin simply disappears. Sexuality and death can be confronted more directly. The God of Islam may have mercy or weakness, but these are subordinated to strength. Allah is uniformly just, but this does not prevent him from exercising reward and punishment on earth. Man's lot is obedience to a powerful, transcendent God who has power everywhere, and who will reward obedience. The current transcendence of God is coded in the fact of Muhammad's final revelation, after which a personal or mediated relationship to God is moot. The concepts involved in this picture do not seem to translate easily into Western concepts. God's omnipotence means that he is powerful everywhere and can do what he wishes everywhere, rather than meaning literally that he can do anything whatsoever. The emphasis is on the fact that he can do whatever he needs and wants to do, not on whether he can do anything *conceivable*, a problem that can arise only in a more abstract philosophical context. As with other Eastern religions, patterns of concrete argumentation tend not to reach the level of logical abstraction that is the legacy of Greek philosophy. Reason exists to permit obedience, rather than to allow an understanding of God.

The doctrine of Islam is coupled with an emphasis on poetic and behavioral expression, and the result, while it issues in complex theological positions, is somewhere between the doctrinal permissiveness of Hinduism and Christian exclusivity.[18] Pillars of the faith include the recital of the word, a public evidence of submission to Allah, the performance of prayer, the giving of alms, fasting, and pilgrimage to Mecca (which can more recently be accomplished by a proxy). Holy war is permitted for defensive purposes only, and is touched by restrictions on barbarity. Tolerance within Islamic areas is supported by the sacred writings, which include the books of Moses, the Psalms of David, and the Gospel of Jesus along with the Quran. The Quran, of course, is God's final revelation superseding the somewhat corrupt earlier texts in any matter of dispute. God (Allah), the angels (including Gabriel), and twenty-eight prophets (including Muhammad, Moses, David, and Jesus) complete the higher ontology, and Islam accepts a final judgment, resurrection of the body, and heaven and hell. The more optional doctrine of Kismet can be interpreted fatalistically, but often simply interprets the extent of Allah's power to permit him to allow events of which he does not fully approve. Relative paucity of structure allows Islamic theology to be easily adapted to local situations, an important factor in its spread that is somewhat different from the complex doctrinal variations of Christianity.

We have earlier described religion as represented by values that seem imposed, and that can be used to give guidance to action, especially forms of social protest. Religions obviously differ from other belief systems in terms of their scope. Their account of significance and correct action, at least in theory, should be able to permeate all a believer's attitudes, beliefs, and actions. A theory of openings in chess is not a religion, although it may be normative in guiding a choice of moves; it only applies to the chess opening. Marxism has the appropriate scope and features to be considered a religion. Marxism presents an analysis of a person's place in society and of how one should act in society based not on knowledge of transcendent beings, but on the social and psychological consequences of the relationships that people have established in societies as producers and consumers of goods. This is conjoined with a historical orientation that is somewhat similar to those we have already studied, except that people are enjoined to achieve heaven on earth in the form of the classless society through intensified human effort. Rather than anticipating an afterlife, Marxism argues that its analysis provides a blueprint for immediate action to bring this better society about.[19] No doubt the appeal of Marxism is partly precisely that improvement in the human condition does not require transcendental mediation, but can be achieved here and now by ourselves.

Perhaps it is no longer controversial among philosophers interested in religion to count Marxism as a religion because of these features. Classic early objections to Marxism (Durkheim's, Weber's) center on the suggestion that the Marxist construal of human nature in terms of economic relationships is partial and reductionistic. Religion, or the structure of society itself, may be a partial determinant of economic structure, so that the play of causal relationships is more complex than it seems in Marx's vision, or simple causal versions of that vision.[20] In any event, the scope of the opposed versions is an indicator that Marxism is ap-

propriately treated as a religion, and by so taking it we have the
possibility that a uniform theory of religion applicable to all current
societies may yet be worked out.

Interestingly enough, the picture of the classless society offered
by Marxism is in many ways as vague and empty as the description
of heaven, say, in Christianity. It can be said of the classless society
that the true nature of human beings will develop without restric-
tion there and that each one will find total happiness and fulfillment. But this raises more questions than one can solve. Is there
a uniform true nature of human beings merely distorted in capitalism, or will human beings be completely different in the classless
society? If there is a true nature, it is not clear that actual human
beings on earth could sufficiently conquer aggressiveness and envy
so as to permit some form of total cooperation.[21] On the other
hand, if the notion of individuality underlying these problems is
dropped, and humans in the classless society will not be at all like
us, how can we anticipate that it will be heaven on earth? Why
should one accept its coming fatalistically, or even abet its birth?
Here Marxism encounters deeper motivational restrictions, which
is no doubt why local praxis generally concentrates on the elimination of evils already present in some specific capitalist complex.

Structurally, versions of Marxism can be as close to forms of
Christianity or Judaism as one can conceive except for their drop-
ping of the notion of original sin and the fact that they recognize no
divine being. In a curious way, the course of history itself replaces
God, as God may be immanent in a universe in which he does not
appear in various religious systems. If the working out of historical
processes is inevitable, then perhaps history is in a confrontation
with the concept of human freedom as acute as the confrontation
between God's nature and human free will, except that there is no
agency to permit free will. Should chance play a role, or if human
freedom can determine (even if only at times) the course of history,
there is no guarantee that the classless society must come, and the
problem of local strategy, attempting to meliorate the bad features
of a society that functions to some degree, but imperfectly, exhausts
the vision of the future. Working directly toward revolution, purge,

and total change, comes to be replaced by an attempt to hit closer targets in a context of more diffuse visions of the future. Praxis and theory become uncoupled as one awaits more certain knowledge. One finds warring Marxist sects whose doctrinal disputes mirror the vicious and repressive confrontations between Christian sects; and both wars can be traced to disputes over contradictory belief systems. Belief rather than praxis determines orthodoxy. Should one wait or act? It depends on a correct reading of the situation. And action itself may become less problematic than the reasons for action, where reasons are related to a correct derivation from canonized text.

Hinduism seems to have resulted from the mingling of religious ideas of two cultures: an indigenous Indian culture and an Aryan culture associated with Aryan invaders who entered India about 2000 B.C. The earliest Hindu scriptures are mostly Aryan in their ideas (the Vedas), but Hinduism as a whole, especially the ideas associated with the Upanishads and the Bhagavad Gita, exhibit an apparent resurfacing of ideas from the indigenous population. On the whole, the population of India was not mobile except for the movements of these conquering armies, and Hinduism is, as a theological system, imposed on an enormous variety of local practices involving local gods and shrines. A person involved in local practices may never encounter the inconsistency between this practice and other local practices, and where Hindu thinkers are aware of it, the variance can be ascribed to the complexity of manifestation that may be attributed to the higher gods. The sheer variety of belief encompassed within Hinduism, and tolerated within Hinduism, may have something to do with the fundamental idea that the world is an illusion.

Unlike any of the other major religions we are looking at, Hinduism has no known human founder. There is no God making a founding revelation through a prophet, nor any human figure who plays a prophetic role like that of Moses in Judaism or Muhammad in Islam. There is no specific sacred text or set of texts to which proper belief is normally to be traced. There are, however, philosophies of Hinduism that sharply disagree and may or may not be

monistic; for example, Hinduism is generally relative in its epistemology. All revelation is partial truth; and the sacred penetrates
everywhere. Some texts are more worthwhile to study; but no
sharp line around canonical scripture is drawn. The complexity of
the universe (which is undoubtedly illusory as it presents itself to
us) can't be reduced by the human mind to a manageable set of
generalities, except perhaps partially for technological purposes.
Hinduism is a religion in which representations of various gods, all
of whom stand for partial understandings of the universe, are permitted; and there is no prohibition on images as there is in Judaism
and Islam.

Very basic notions in Hinduism (and Buddhism) are quite divergent from Western notions of individuality and action. Individuals
are who they are by birth, but also as a consequence of activities in
previous existences, which determine to some extent their status at
birth.[22] The boundary of individuality, which in our terms is a location for a unitary person who thinks and interprets the world and
then acts on his or her interpretation, is not a real boundary in
Hinduism, but an illusory one that is ultimately responsible for
human error and suffering. Hinduism presents a picture of the
human personality more akin to that presented by psychoanalytic
theory than by popular culture. Warring and conflicting tendencies
operate, caused partly by reductive analyses of the surrounding
world. The object is to achieve a state where these tendencies no
longer operate and self-control is achieved in the sense that the
world no longer manipulates the self through reductive interaction.
In a sense, a state is reached where the boundary of the self is obscure, or even erased. The presupposition that this process can
occur is that the perfectability of human beings is limitless, a presupposition totally at odds with the notion of original sin in Christianity, and perhaps ultimately at odds with the notion of sin and
a single lifetime of judgment in its associated religions.

From this point of view, we can look at the doctrine of detachment. Hindu philosophers are very subtle in the analysis of human
perception and action, as their philosophies are ultimately directed
toward self-control, rather than primarily toward morality or intel-

lectual understanding. The appropriate form of self-control can be practiced within the boundaries of self already mentioned by preserving some sense of connectedness. Hindu psychologists had noticed long ago that there is no choice between acting and non-acting, because not acting is itself an action that may have consequences as dramatic as anything normally considered to be positive action.[23] Similarly, any person with a rule of action is chained to features of the external world.[24] One who regularly smokes is just as chained to smoking as one who does not, one who never smokes. Signals from the outside world are managed by an inflexible policy, or a lapse from that policy, and consequent guilt or sorrow. We may see the world as impinging on us in terms of digital stimuli to which we can appropriately react by finding the right set of rules. Hindu consciousness rather sees stimuli as analogue and incredibly complex, to which one must appropriately react by subtle modulated feelings, since the structure of rules and generalizations is too crude for reality. The detached person has set rules of conduct to one side. He or she may or may not smoke, depending on the subtlety of circumstances, and will certainly not presume in advance that smoking is inherently good or bad, or that there is some appropriate action linked to generally describable circumstances by a rule of conduct. Habits, of course, are suspect, and must be broken, even if they are, relatively speaking, good habits for most situations. The detached soul is not an impartial observer, but a completely committed observer, looking at all of the details of a situation from the unique point of view determined by individual history. Complete self-control results in spontaneous action, action geared precisely to the unique situation at hand. No practical syllogism can properly intervene, that is, an inference from facts in the situation to what it is that we should do.

All of this may seem strange to us, although it has been presented here in a way that attempts to stress its possible rationality in our terms. Nonetheless, there seems to be a built-in bias toward passivity. First, we can dismiss the idea that the temptation is to accumulate information before acting, because information doesn't lead to action, and one is painfully conscious that one is not acting while accumulating information, with all the attendant problems of not acting. But now let us consider taking some dramatic action, such as making war against other people, or building a temple. Should these be within one's power? As expressions of self, these are almost certain to meet with failed expectations, and pain and sorrow in consequence, and it is hard to work out the actual consequences and circumstances in which one would find them appropriate if one is detached. Further, these actions will have a large effect on others, and constitute awkward constraints on their actions. It's hard to see how they wouldn't lead to some additional human misery, even if they lead to additional human joy, but the future is difficult to read. Not acting is most likely to feel right in many cases; and withdrawal or renunciation, the best form of control, because it doesn't involve complicated interaction with others. But if everyone were to withdraw, society would come to a standstill. In the end, then, the caste system, even though it is a point of attack for religions splitting from Hinduism, provides a neat solution to the problem of action, since it apportions the actions required for the continuance of society to various groups under various conditions, while not excluding anyone from salvation because of the associated doctrine of transmigration.

There are four basic genera in the classic caste system, which can be analyzed as having four strategies associated with them for the manipulation of earthly and spiritual goods.[25] The highest caste (Brahman) may receive earthly goods from members of other castes, but only highly purified or prepared goods, goods that can then be transformed in the subtle spiritual code. In a sense, the division of labor in the caste system includes a division of religious labor, the Brahman acquiring spiritual knowledge, achieving release or self-control, and perhaps dispensing advice and religious teaching to members of lower castes. Members of lower castes cannot afford, and do not have the natures making it possible for them to participate in, the higher spiritual practices. Their attitudes toward things and other people must be partially alienated in conformity with the exigencies of survival. Higher attitudes will treat other people not possessively, but in a spirit of respect. Everyone is

bound together in the caste system. It may be a general's appropriate action to fight a battle, and if this causes additional pain, that
may be balanced by the achievement of release from bondage for
persons who might not otherwise have achieved it. Further, as some
of each of us is to be found in all of us, and persons are not divided
so neatly into separate individuals, the achievement of release by
anyone is a potential victory for all. Lower caste members have the
possibility of overcoming bad karma and bringing about a better
stage in the next cycle, so everyone is potentially involved in the
spiritual process.

There are, of course, distinct strategies possible for achieving
release. Paths differ in terms of their emphasis on proper religious
activity (performances of rites, etc.), devotion, or meditation
directed toward insight or contemplation. The last form has proved
most appealing to Western philosophers, since it obviously can be
related to philosophical contemplation in the West, and has, in fact,
given rise to Hindu philosophical systems.

Buddhism was originally a version of Hinduism, one rejecting
the caste system in its traditional setting. Its founder (Siddhartha or
Gautama) lived in India in the early years of the sixth century B.C.,
but rejected Hinduism and many of its associated ideas. One can
consider Buddhism as a missionary, universalist form of Hinduism,
somewhat analogous to the way in which Christianity can be considered a missionary, universalist form of Judaism. Many of the
same religious ideas permeate both religions, but Buddhism breaks
the hold of the caste system and the set of actions proper to members of the various estates. Buddhism offers salvation or release to
anyone willing to follow its truths and disciplines. There is a focus
on the elimination of pain and suffering, and a removal of divine
agency from the world. In Hinduism, God is in the world (or gods,
depending on the version), but Buddhism rejects this sort of immanence, perhaps because of an intolerance for the idea that gods
could be associated with a world where pain and suffering is so
obvious.

Buddhism is not rooted to a cultural area, as Hinduism is, but it
has been introduced into, and takes forms peculiar to, the various

areas in which it is found. As the official religion in some of these areas, it comes into protracted conflict with less pacific indigenous religious forms. Where Hinduism has a sort of biological flavor, and many local gods who are heroes, mothers, lovers, or whatever, Buddhism has a more patristic, psychological flavor. In all forms, Buddhism emphasizes compassion, meditation, and a struggle against illusion. This may partially account for its attractiveness to dissident Western intellectuals.

The Buddha was originally a wealthy member of a higher caste, but on pleasure trips with his charioteer, he was impressed by seeing age, suffering, agony, and death. He became fixated with the thought that the early joy of life ends before its dreams can be fulfilled on earth, suggesting that the meaning of life must lie elsewhere. Perhaps the Buddha's atheism sprang from the denial of Hinduism's belief that God is in the world, since these observations suggest that the world is not good and doesn't contain God. After a period of renunciation, he accepted the idea that suffering is caused by desire, and can be eliminated by eliminating desire, a process to be accomplished in Buddhism by the eightfold path. An important insight is that the self/other dichotomy is an illusion, and that the self is a complicated interaction of five principles, an interaction that leaves a permanent impress on the universe, and that sets up subtle negative reflections from the universe back onto any person not tuned correctly to its structure. But at death, the principles separate, so that it is not literally true that souls pass from body to body in the transmigration cycle.

Although the caste system is overtly abandoned, it should be noted that religions that have a distinction between a priesthood and a laity, or some similar distinctions, possess a form of caste, and Buddhism is no exception. One might say that the division of labor is imperfect outside Hinduism, in the sense that the interactions of priest and follower are not mediated by the subtle codes of transaction for gross and subtler goods which characterize Hinduism. The less the distinction between monk and layperson, as in Mahayana Buddhism, the more the religion becomes universalistic. The Buddha is a teacher, and one need not leave the world on achieving release. Everything is interrelated, self and other, and the person who has achieved release stays in this world as a teacher. More exclusive forms, as in Theravada Buddhism, tend to emphasize the distinction between monk and layperson, and to upgrade the purity of release. Clearly, the interaction of caste with the religious principles of Hinduism results in a complicated Buddhist dialectic of change when the caste system is altered by the imposition of a negative judgment concerning its acceptability.

3

Religion and Social Issues

CHAPTER ANALYSIS   In this chapter we examine the relationship between theological belief and specific social critique. The point of this examination is to establish the conjecture that specific critique, specific belief, or specific action is not derived from theological belief as theorem is derived from axiom, but is a construction utilizing theological resources to legitimate an attitude that may seem forced onto one by factual considerations. Theologies provide building blocks and attitudes, but not completely detailed belief except in specially constructed systems. Divergent theologians may thus be related like wave and particle theorists in the history of science, opponents prepared to accommodate detailed fact with theories that may become interchangeable at the local level if facts tend to force agreement. Views of religion that emphasize fixed rules, such as the Ten Commandments, or fixed theological systems, as the core of religion, are thus forcing a misleading epistemological confrontation. We concentrate here on four topics: evil, environmental issues, war, and the status of women. With respect to evil, which is perhaps the most abstract problem, the traditions contain resources for active opposition or passive accommodation to specifically recognized evils, in spite of apparent differences at the theological level concerning the philosophical question of the existence of evil and its nature. With respect to environmental issues, attitudes favoring change or conservation can be justified in all the traditions, even if specific notions of what constitutes change may take on cultural specificity. With respect to war, the traditions are in agreement that a notion of just war can be developed to distinguish legitimate from illegitimate taking of life. With respect to the status of women, even if the traditions have generally accepted the prevailing social difference in status for men and women, they also contain the resources to urge greater inequality or complete equality, providing a range of critical perspectives on the actual status of women in society. My survey of these four issues is designed to give content to the possibility of religion as critique, and to establish that the possibility of specific critique is always available when theology and social prejudice confront one another. This fact cannot be accounted for by the ahistorical philosophical picture of religion as a belief system, or any simple sociological theory of religion as a reflection of social structure.

THE last chapter looked at some very general features of the theologies associated with major contemporary religions. We have seen that four of these religions have a natural historical linkage, as does the remaining pair. Only the most general features of these theologies relevant to our later discussion have been noted, and it has been stressed that these general theologies take on a huge variety of appropriate local forms. This has been part of the claim defended here that religions form a source of critical ideas that can be applied to particular social formations. If this claim is true, the idea that religion is outmoded falsehood, or that it is a mere symbolic expression of surrounding society, cannot be true for the major contemporary religions.

Some have proposed that religion is a sheer fantasy designed to make life on earth more tolerable, and that religion survives from the past as a means of expressing wish fulfillment in the present. This may be advanced for permissive forms of contemporary religion, but hardly seems an accurate total account. When we look at the doctrine of hell, for example, it hardly seems the sort of thing that would be developed to make life on earth more pleasant, particularly in the historical form in which hell threatens believers themselves, and not just pagans. Orthodox versions of the religions have established an onerous and dangerous regimen to connect belief with salvation. It seems clear that religion invests life with significance, rather than with compensation. A convert to any major religion may well find his or her past life judged harshly, and worry considerably about achieving a life that measures up to the new standards. One does not convert to feel better, but, at least sometimes, to have a basis for criticizing others and the surrounding society, in terms of insights that secular accommodation to power cannot justify.

The fact that the major religions take on so many varied forms in national and local contexts also rebuts any easy idea that religion merely reflects society. It can be the case that certain kinds of society will be associated with certain major types of religion, but it is pointless to abstract at this level.[1] Quite different societies express attachment to the same major religion, often on historical grounds, but the religion will typically receive distinct local coloring. This is what would be expected if the religions were repositories of critical resources, since they could quite easily be adapted to local circumstances. Further, one might expect conflict between forms of the same religion within the same society on this basis. Of course, society may be internally in conflict, or even contradictory. If religion is a reflection of society, this situation should cause projection of blatantly contradictory religions. More likely, opposed interests may use a relatively consistent religious system to articulate their own interests into a privatized form of religion. This is what is found. For example, as we will note below, arguments for and against the wearing of the veil by Muslim women will be based on religious considerations. Religion, while it transcends the individual, as does society, cannot simply reflect society. It provides a means of articulating one's perception of society, which entails at least some potential divergence from total societal norms if special features of the society are to be noticed and developed.

Let us consider the biblical text, for a moment. No one simply reading the text could possibly guess at the positions concerning such topics as evil, war, and the status of women that are actually adopted by self-confessed Christians, nor perhaps at their variety. One of the problems in interpreting at least some other religions is that we are tied down to text due to the physical impossibility of internalizing all the contemporary forms of the great religions. Who could guess, for example, based on the general antipathy expressed between Christians and Marxists (based on the question of atheism), that some thinkers have seen these movements as natural allies, at least under the current interpretation?[2] To agree that Buddhists must be, or even should be, pacifistic, because of what the Buddha said, is to travel the parallel past from Christ's sayings to pacifistic Christian behavior. All of this would overlook historical interpretation, and in particular the development of various notions of justified violence that seems to have been thrust on the large religions by virtue of their association with civil power. In this chapter, we will study some of the consequences for social issues of the major theologies, starting with the somewhat abstract problem of evil, but then turning to the more concrete and related problems of war and the status of women. As we move toward the concrete, we will notice in every case an increasing complexity of expression, a fact that is consistent with the picture of the role of the major religions that is being defended here.

The problem of reconciling God's nature with the existence of evil seems virtually unique to Christianity and those religions dependent upon Christianity. For the Jews, there were problems about suffering, and the way in which it was distributed in the world, but suffering itself is not intrinsically bad. Suffering may ennoble the sufferer, and it seems compatible with the nature of God, who suffers when his good intentions are thwarted by human misconduct. Let us look at the distribution problem. Suffering does not seem correlated to merit on the individual level, therefore it seems to require theological treatment. Standard answers to this problem are developed in Judaism.[3] Suffering may be attached to nations. For example, some of the prophets argued that the Jews had suspended the original Covenant through misbehavior, and Jewish suffering was a preparatory step for recognition and acceptance of a new Covenant. It was also argued that suffering and merit were proportional, but retribution might be delayed. This was hard to work out historically in Judaism because of the absence of clear Jewish belief in heaven and hell, but the possibility had a strong impact on Christian theology. It could also be argued that suffering is simply misunderstood by human beings, who are able to fathom only part of the complexity and grandeur of God's creation. Job is often interpreted this way, and this is a way of dealing with suffering (and evil) that is later accepted by some Christian theologians. These answers are all logically possible, but not conclusive. One wishes to know more, and in some respects later Christian theology attempts to satisfy that impulse.

Perhaps the most interesting answer, however, is one that did not pass into the Christian tradition, and that cannot pass into any religion that is based on a strong notion of individuality. This answer is the instantiation of the ennobling effects of suffering. Suffering can be a *test* of faith, as a trial designed by God to test the worth of a particular human being for some divine purpose. In particular, the sufferings of one person may make up for the sins of others, and the sufferings of one nation may reconcile God to the totality of his creation, especially the bad behavior of other nations. The latter notion has been important in Jewish history, but we shall concentrate on the former idea. Technically, this possibility is coded into the notion of atonement, the notion that one person (through suffering) can *atone for* the sins of others. Atonement can only work where a strong shared community is presupposed, where there are corporate personalities in some sense. Does the fault or sin of one family member reflect on the entire family? Do the sins of the father become visited on his offspring? If so, human personalities are not totally distinct, and one person can stand in for another. In priestly versions, animal sacrifice or burnt offering can atone at least for the unintentional violations of covenant.[4] And, of course, the suffering of the exile can atone for the earlier sins of the Jews. Where people are autonomous, the idea of atonement is meaningless, or must be given some weakened "symbolic" interpretation. One can answer only for one's own sins.

The modern attachment of Christianity to cultures where autonomy of personality is dominant has lost this very beautiful notion, without which Jesus' death must receive a symbolic or allegorical treatment. In early Christianity, the doctrine of atonement would have retained its original meaning, the tremendous personal suffering of Jesus atoning for people's sins, allowing reconciliation of God and man. This idea must be painfully and explicitly translated into our forms of consciousness in order to become comprehensible. Even in the modern Jewish Day of Atonement, one recounts one's past sins, and throws oneself on God's mercy, without necessarily invoking resonance with this older idea of atonement. As we shall see, this is partly an accommodation involving the modernization of Judaic theology in a Christian, and largely Protestant, social setting.

The original idea of atonement resurfaces throughout history. For example, the Holocaust can be seen as atonement, but also as a refutation of the religion, or as a terrible retribution (like the Flood) for desertion of the Covenant. All these approaches (and others) have been expressed by Jewish authors. The Holocaust is a surd in history (like Naziism itself, or the Jonestown suicides), an event where transcendent impingement seems as reasonable an explanation as any in view of there being no coherent explanation in terms of current historical science. To attempt superficial explanation would be to bring these events into history as though they were capable of a smooth fit in the linear flow of other events. They are not; and we shall leave them as abruptly as they were mentioned, as signposts to a legitimate notion of transcendence.

The idea of suffering as ennobling came into popular Christianity from Judaism as the appropriate form of Christian appearance on earth: the imitation of Christ. Many Christians, including poorer Christians into the twentieth century, have adopted the example of Christ as providing the appropriate model for the renunciation of worldly goods and the service of others. Christ's life ended in an apparent defeat (only the Christian knew of the secret victory), while Moses and Muhammad, for example, were successful as earthly leaders. Imitation of Christ is a special form of Christian "folly," and a special way of treating suffering based on concrete example. Monastic orders have drawn from this course throughout history, a point of contact with Buddhism, and make very little rational sense except against this background. Uproar against the opulence and circumstances of the official Church based on the nature of Christ's life is a central aspect of the Protestant Reformation, a movement whose most successful branches have repeated the climb to acceptance, accommodation, and wealth. But the fact of success cannot be avoided. Within the Christian churches that succeeded, theologians were interested in the puzzles brought by the amalgamation of Greek philosophy with Judaic theological insights. Suffering was not the central experience of these theologians; rather the problem of reconciling the abstract nature of God with the abstract fact of evil in the world. The two branches of Christian concern indicate sufficiently the problem confronting any attempt at unified explanation.

We have looked at the problem of reconciliation in the first chapter from the standpoint of abstract rationality, but some remarks are necessary here about the development of evil. Sin is the mere doing of something defined as wrong by the judgment of divine command, a state of affairs known to most religions. Sin can perhaps be made up or expunged in various ways. The sinner may feel remorse, shame, guilt, regret, and may wish to repent, change course, and avoid similar lapses in the future. Evil is a harder notion. An evil person in some sense knowingly does wrong, and has no regrets about it until punishment becomes involved, and perhaps not even then. In Christianity, God makes the sacrifice of his son to redeem human sin, a sacrifice that is both ultimate and infinite. Because of the proofs associated with the divinity of Christ, rejection of this message within orthodox Christianity is an infinite crime, because it is the rejection of an infinitely loving gift. Evil in the world we will understand as arising from actions taken by evil persons in the world. A transcendent aspect of life is inevitably conjured up by the shift from sin to evil, and this shift is intrinsic to historical, orthodox Christianity.

The infinite crime conjured up within Christianity by rejection of Christ ultimately called forth an appropriate concept of hell. Many early theologians were in dispute about the nature of hell and the length of time it might last, at least one major approach arguing that God's goodness was incompatible with an eternal hell.[5] Orthodox hell gradually developed into the doctrine familiar in Christian folklore. Fear of hell became, sometimes quite consciously manipulated by theologians, a deterrent to evil action and thought in this life. The happiness of those in heaven was reported to come from their enjoyment in seeing the torments of the damned.[6] These views were supported by such prominent theologians as Augustine and Aquinas, but they have declined in importance in modern times. Philosophically, however, the problem of infinite punishment for an infinite crime remains. As the body can only take or feel a finite quantity of pain at any given time, only infinitely long torment can add up to infinite punishment, so that hell's infinity can be supported conceptually by arguments independent of the scriptural sources. This was all wrapped up by such theologians as Tobias Swinden, who felt confident in determining the number of the damned per square mile (100 billion), and located hell in the sun, whose fires in the Copernican universe were as far from heaven as possible and could be expected to last forever.[7]

When hell is clearly articulated in some such way, the problem of the distribution of evil and suffering (granted that the theodicy permits its existence) has a retributive solution that can satisfy any demands for a bookkeeping of evil, and this is one form of the classical Christian solution. Within Christianity, there are fragmented versions of all the Judaic solutions, such as the unintelligibility of God's ways. These have had a resuscitation in modern times, when the doctrine of hell and some of its associated terrors has been downplayed in the effort to attract new adherents to the religion. In fact, damnation, which is involved with the doctrine of original sin and infinite hell, as well as the claim, supported clearly by biblical texts, that the ratio of damned to saved is extremely high, has proved awkward for churches accommodating increasing secular power, and has been softened or dropped.

Islam provides no new conceptual resources for considering the problem of evil. God becomes even more transcendent, losing the carefully circumscribed properties that made him accessible in Christian theology. It is the power of God that is stressed in Islam, and the awful consequences of not submitting to his will. There are some parallels here between Calvinism and Islam, partly signaled by Calvinism's ban (unusual in Christianity) on visual representations of God. God is mysterious because he is so powerful; and to some extent he loses personal interest in human beings, judging them by rule rather than by exception. In Islam, of course, establishing direct communication with God is impossible, a fact associated with his greater transcendence. The transcendence implies that incomprehension is the major Islamic solution for the existence of evil in God's world, freeing one to attend to the circumstances of one's own earthly life, whereas the partial intelligibility of the future led to discipline toward heaven in Calvinism.

Between Marxism and Christianity there are a number of apparent gulfs, notably in their quite different basic opinions about human nature. Christianity is unique in its (theoretical) pessimism toward human nature; in some versions in its insistence that people will always be involved with evil thoughts and action. This view is weakened in Islam, and completely done away with in Marxism, where evil is the consequence of bad social and economic arrangements which will be entirely overcome, or at least *can* be overcome, by enlightened human action. The problem of evil, so to speak, has a mechanical solution in Marxism. Its existence seems to require no transcendent source, and its elimination is also a matter of events entirely within this world, so that evil itself becomes problematic, and the problems are centrally those of pain and suffering. The appeal of Marxism is in its optimistic call to action. We can eliminate pain and suffering and evil; let's get to it. But disenchantment often takes the form of questioning whether Marxism hasn't forgotten some depressing constancies concerning human nature. One version of this remembers Freud's pessimism regarding the ultimate compatibility of the self with any social structure, and attempts to work out a Freud-Marx synthesis based on a more pessimistic analysis of human nature coupled with a Marxism emphasizing human thought, action, and historical uncertainty.[8] Another version returns to Judaic roots, and finds the difficulty in Christianity's attempt to explain or justify evil, reducing it unexpectedly to a secular phenomenon. Old Testament prophets give no explanations; they simply *denounce* evil. In this light, the Fall of Adam and Eve may not be a fall from innocence based on wickedness, but a fall into wickedness based on innocence, based on not noticing evil, based on wanting to try something different.[9] Perhaps the thought that evil can be eradicated is ultimately incoherent, evil being an essential aspect of this world. We must simply oppose evil: that is the divine injunction. Oppose it not because there is a reason to oppose it, but because it is a duty. This attitude also demands action to replace the hesitation of philosophy, action based on the idea that we can discern the evil in front of us while philosophy is involved in the outlines of the classless future.

What is common to the monotheistic sequence of religions is the idea that a good world is possible containing human beings recognizable to us, here on earth now, or here on earth in the future, or in heaven. A common structural problem is that of dealing with the fact that a good God or good humans could have created a world with pain and suffering in it, distributed in the way that it seems to be. This problem, to some extent, simply disappears in Hinduism and Buddhism. Perhaps conflict within a polytheistic setting explains partially why this is so, but the world is simply seen as essentially the place where pain and suffering occur. Rather than changing the world, one withdraws from it. Further, the gods cannot help, for insofar as they are various, they repeat the confusions of the world in their interaction. Monistic systems support this sense of illusion, since the apparent world is sacred, but unstable and temporary. Problems of distribution of pain and suffering, of course, are neatly solved in the transmigration cycle, since status is simply the consequence of past history plus current achievement of control of one's ascribed status. There is no way for humans to eradicate pain and suffering, or to live where pain and suffering have been eradicated, since living and pain and suffering are co-referential. The individual must disappear.

Thus far we have looked at theoretical responses to the sheer existence of pain, suffering, and evil on earth. Specific injustices causing these may be confronted in an active or passive manner; all the major religions contain the resources for both responses, in spite of variations in their theoretical positions on individuality. We had, during the Vietnam War, the passive self-immolation of Buddhist monks who were unwilling to confront violence to others with violence to others. But, of course, Christ's injunction to turn the other cheek can produce nonviolent adaptations to violence as well, and even sacrifice of oneself can be integrated into the total theological framework of Christianity, with obvious parallels to Christ's own death. When we turn to more specific problems, the same dizzying repertoire of possible versions of the major religions gives considerable pause as to the linkage between religion and surrounding society. Accommodating versions may simply attempt to justify prevailing social practice, but critical versions of considerable variety will be available within the conceptual resources offered by the religion. We will look at three topics—mankind's relationship to the environment, to war, and to the treatment of women—in an effort to study this more closely.

Human beings have modified nature throughout their history, sometimes in ways harmful both to themselves and to nature. Recently, the possibility that this may have been done, or is being done, on a scale that can threaten the continued existence of human life has been explicitly discussed in Western countries. In some quarters, the blame has been placed squarely on Christianity, as a religion that is supportive of independence from, and control of, natural surroundings. This position is somewhat athwart the thrust of the suggestion that Christianity is the bulwark of social conservatism, and that it has been the bitter enemy of science and progress. Given the complexity of positions possible within Christianity, there is no reason to suppose that Christianity might not have played both roles until more history is considered. And, of course, the positions can be easily reconciled by observing that the blame for pollution, that is the *misuse* of science, can be shifted from science to religion by this maneuver.[10]

Science and associated technology have given human beings the augmented power to destroy the environment possibly beyond any repair, thus terminating human life. But this capacity might be utilized anywhere, and its attractiveness is shown by the rapid acceptance of science and technology in non-Christian areas of the world. The desire to control the environment and the advantages of doing so are as old as recorded history in all traditions. Marxism, in most of its forms, does not intend to give up the powers of science, but means simply to bend them to the purposes of another social structure and a theoretically more even pattern of distribution. Social forces calling for control and exploitation of nature have existed in all human societies; their implementation in modern times is simply more dramatic in terms of its potential consequences. If Christianity and pragmatism are both components of our culture, why should Christianity be blamed for this situation? Could it even be that it is the weakening of Christianity that allows this situation to become increasingly problematic?[11]

Christianity becomes an obscure target. Christianity is much older than the environmental crisis and much older than effective modern science. At the start, it was opposed to the worldly focus required for science, and later independent of science, as we have seen in our survey of current attitudes. The current division of domain may represent a retreat from older Christian doctrines about nature as God's creation, or nature as a text revelatory of God, but except for this negative freedom that Christianity allows scientifically aided exploitation, Christianity cannot be said to foment the rape of the environment. This standoff is a matter of record. The new plowing methods of the seventh century, vital to the developing domination of nature and increasing populations, were developed, as was much of the vital technological thrust of the Middle Ages, by persons not schooled in theology, who regarded this as a practical matter. Praising God for such developments, where it might have occurred, cannot be taken as forging a link between theology and the shape of a plow, but instead as a religious expression of gratitude for more abundant harvests. It is hard to see that more abundant harvests would not be praised in other cultural traditions. It can be said that Christianity may have played a role in the development of early modern science in Europe, a Christian crucible, but it can hardly be blamed for what is happening now if science is not also to be involved in the condemnation as a separate institution.

Science seems to have been the product of multiple causes. There is a record of science going back to the Greeks, but it was then associated with an elitist, philosophical approach to reasoning about nature, which is no doubt in the form of theory essential to the development of modern scientific theory. But science requires the fusion of this cerebral attitude with experimentation and involvement with natural processes, an aspect developed by the trial-and-error intuitive technologists of the medieval period. Modern, potentially catastrophic developments result from augmenting science and technology with vast sums of government and private monies which can be spent to implement scientific and technical schemes. The Christian religion was not looking, and only reacted to these developments, although the developing independence of church and state in Europe may have created the space in which science could develop. The Greek East, with Christianity, did not develop science.[12] But science also needs a mathematics that can be applied to nature, a mathematics that was, in fact, developed within Islamic culture. Science accelerated in Protestant countries, where potentially oppositional but adopted secular and sacred institutions fragmented into institutions expressing more private interests. But there is a scale of Protestantisms as well, from Calvin's experiment with a highly controlled Geneva to perfectly wild marginal cults. It can be that Protestantism interiorizes Christianity, forcing its circumscription within the private sphere, permitting the public sphere to be ruled by explicitly independent pragmatic criteria, but neither science nor capitalism is easily traced to a specifically Protestant cause. In any event, it is Christianity and not Protestantism that is blamed, very few writers suggesting that a Catholic country might have greater conceptual resources for defending the environment. Further, an implicational argument could single out Judaism, as we would not have Christianity without Judaism, and yet this is one thing that the Jews are not blamed for in current scholarly debates. The attack on Christendom seems here to have some clear ideological component.

The contrast of Christianity with Eastern religions seems a case of orientalism, oversimplifying the contrasting religions to develop an oppositional stance from oversimplified points of origin. Much has been made of a Buddhist reluctance to disturb snakes in building roads.[13] Stories of concerned Buddhists are, to be sure, a way of gaining perspective on the impact of our technology, but the situation is not simple. Buddhist and Hindu road builders must often consider local religions in the process of larger social works, local religions of the kind that Christianity largely eradicated in Europe in conjunction with increasingly powerful state apparatuses. Further, the fit of a road to its environment is partly a function of the monies that can be spent per mile, the cheapest road entailing the least change in the environment where the terrain is difficult. The gap between ideology and practice can be shown in non-Christian areas by examples that are tempered only by lack of technological means, deforestation in particular being common at various times and places in areas represented by all the major religions.[14] Further, the Judaic and Christian traditions contain no worship of artisan gods, as there is in other traditions, and do contain such stories as those of Francis of Assisi and his redemptive relationship to animals. Major religions seem, in fact, not to entail *any* particular attitude toward the natural environment. Current concern may well be based on special current class considerations, and quite independent of the content of particular theologies.[15] Why is religion pulled this way and that on such issues, and why is it invoked? It seems most likely that certain secular problems that become important (for whatever reason) but resist secular solution call for religious reference. There is no particular reason to believe that Christianity should be rationally singled out as responsible for the end of human life should human life be snuffed out by uncontrollable Western pollution. Changes in the environment are not necessarily destructive, and religions are free to select quite differential responses to particular changes. Christians will be found on all sides of current ecological issues, as will the adherents of other religions.

Polytheisms usually have a god of war, and Christ is sometimes referred to as the Prince of Peace. Nonetheless, Christian countries are probably unexcelled (to date) in the pillage and killing of other human beings. This must be tempered by reference to the size of world population, and particularly for the availability of destructive weapons that science has placed in the hands of modern Christian politicians. It is a gloomy proceeding to attempt to guess what the leaders of the past might have done if they had possessed weapons of correspondingly greater destructive power. As the arguments about ecological matters have indicated, there is little to choose between the religions in practice, since all of them provide plenty of resources for advancing peace and plenty of resources for supporting war in associated secular states. Still, more can be said here than can be said about religion and the relationship to nature.

In Hinduism, there is little to inhibit war, since fighting can be appropriate action for members of appropriate castes in appropriate circumstances. The central story line of the Bhagavad Gita, for example, involves the argument that the tentative Arjuna should go into battle because this course of action and the anticipated killing are enjoined by duty. There are, of course, rules of battle not unlike some of those of medieval Christian warfare, such as that certain kinds of soldiers should only be engaged to kill their counterparts in the other army, and not, for example, unarmed civilians. Opposed to this, and passionately advocated by some Hindu sects, is the Hindu doctrine of *ahimsa*, the renunciation of the will to kill or do harm. Ahimsa is based on the sense of unity of the universe, as well as on the fact that committed action (causing harm in this case) would not be based on withdrawal, and would have negative karmic consequences.

Gandhi may be taken as an example of one who pragmatically resolved these doctrines.[16] In his view, suffering animals and dangerous animals might be killed, but enlightened political action should be firm nonviolent action toward positive goals, rather than simple withdrawal. But Gandhi's doctrine of detachment was such that he did not see it as wrong to persevere in violent action for those who could not achieve correct insight into the basis for non-violent action. The consequences of rigid nonviolent action could be as harmful as the consequences of violent action. Gandhi saw means and ends as intrinsically connected, and stressed that selection of means could be controlled by the actor, even if the ultimate consequences of action could not be. Violent means actually chosen to achieve conjectural good ends were simply irrational. In working out his views, he studied the potential for critical distance offered by Christ, Thoreau, Ruskin, and Tolstoy, an instance of the utilization of resources from other traditions for critical perspective. And in turn, Gandhi's synthesis has been drawn on in the West by those interested in the techniques of nonviolent resistance. Gandhi was forced into a symbolic interpretation of the Bhagavad Gita, arguing that the battle under consideration was *within* Arjuna, and that Arjuna is simply being encouraged to act selflessly, a general insight of commanding moral force. This discussion has indicated that Hinduism can provide a spectrum of attitudes, from bellicose to pacific, with compromise between them, the entire spectrum traceable to religious texts. This is more or less the situation to be encountered in the other traditions.

Buddhism's theology stresses a fundamental injunction not to take life, partly based on comparing one's own fear of death with what others may feel, and one's deep attachments to the rest of what exists.[17] But this does not prevent justifications for killing in certain contexts. The preservation and continuance of the Buddha's revelations may be protected by violence, and the Buddha himself is sometimes said to have protected right doctrine by violent means. And killing may be necessary to prevent even greater killing. Moral puzzles are just as available in Buddhist thought as in analytic ethical theory. A Buddhist traveling with 500 others, if warned that 500 bandits are about to attack the caravan by the scout of the bandits, confronts such a problem. If he tells the others, they will kill the scout and take the bandits by surprise, after which they must suffer for taking life. If he doesn't tell the others and does nothing himself, the travelers will be attacked when the scout re-

72

ports back, and lives will be lost. He therefore kills the scout, preventing the attack, and taking the consequences on himself. This is a justified killing. Such ideas may be expanded into versions of the just-war theory, and some Buddhists have even argued that the illusory nature of existence makes killing unreal, so that it does not necessarily entail bad consequences. Although officially pacifistic, and although the Buddha's compassion is the central image of the religion, Buddhism is flexible in local situations, more so than Jainism, for example. It is therefore possible to find in the history of Buddhism the same contradictions that can be found between the image of the Prince of Peace and the shocking behavior of Christian armies in many circumstances.

The historical books of Judaism are filled with battles, and the Jewish God is involved with war in protecting the Promised Land. But there are signs of compassion that become highly developed in the Talmudic tradition. At the end of the book of Jonah, God withholds the destruction of Nineveh out of consideration for its people. The Talmud develops such sources into the idea that deliberate and motivated destruction is a tragic necessity, an occasion for sorrow. Just wars may be fought when there is an attack from the outside, when war may even be obligatory. The Messiah in the context of Judaism was often expected to be a military leader who would shatter the yoke fettering Israel and restore the glories of the kingdom that had existed during the time of David and Solomon.[18]

In Christianity the Messiah is the poignant figure of the King of the Jews who dies on the cross; God's bringing a doctrine of love whose earthly defeat underscores a transcendental triumph. Christian soldiers in the Roman army sometimes refused to fight, or, like Martin of Tours, are said to have entered battle armed only with a cross. But by the time of Constantine, and the close relationship of church and state, one finds the clergy separated from the laity, and the latter expected to fulfill the normal obligations of citizenship. The Church becomes implicated in the success of the Roman army, which is in turn protecting the area where Christianity dominates. Augustine sees war as the instrument of divine judgment on wickedness, interpreting the pacifistic portions of the New Testament as applying primarily to personal relations. Love becomes an inner disposition, and peace is rescued (partially) as the legitimate goal of war.

The medieval period, after the secular defeat of Rome, is racked with wars in spite of lay opinion that war was inconsistent with the New Testament. Popes, curiously, have their own armies, and the Crusades are actually a succession of holy wars. The behavior in the crusader's armies did much to foment Muslim contempt for Christian standards of civility. Gradually the important doctrine of just war is worked out, partially from the monk Gratian's treatise of 1140. Just wars can be fought to repel aggression, or to recover what had been stolen, among other reasons. Immunity is to be granted to such noncombatants as the clergy, women, pilgrims, monks, and the unarmed poor. At the same time, there are countervailing ideas expressed in the life of St. Francis, and more stringent requirements for just war are worked out by Franciscan theologians. In Aquinas, the notion of just war becomes a civil problem for princes who are charged with maintaining the common good.

With the reformation, the situation becomes extremely complex. Some Protestant sects were completely pacifistic, and humanism, impinging on Catholicism, tempered the doctrine of the just war elsewhere, as in Erasmus, who was unable to find any of the wars of his time to be just. At the same time, Protestant states produced armies with Christian chaplains, and the coincidence of religion with local secular aims became more marked. Christian states have participated in the total wars of the twentieth century, and they have been the first whose technology permitted the manufacture and use of modern destructive weaponry. As the potential threat becomes greater, versions of Christian apologetics have been equal to the task. The Second World War was fought partially against non-Christian powers, legitimating force in the service of a dispute whose secular aims were coincident with preserving and extending Christian areas. And currently, Marxist antagonists threaten the existence of Christianity, providing stimulus for new just-war extensions. But in all these cases, Christianity can also deploy a completely pacifistic image, and, on the basis of such images, some Christians have refused to legitimate war.

The secular side of Islam has always invoked the notion of *jihad*, a striving to extend the scope of the Muslim world. This *can* be interpreted as an intellectual striving, for example, but has most prominently been developed as a notion of just war. Original Muslim conquests offered territories about to be invaded a period for peaceful acquiescence, usually three days between the declaration of intent and the commencement of actual fighting, at least in theory. Within Muslim territory, practical toleration was relatively high much of the time. Christians and Jews could retain their faith, and even rise to positions of prominence. Jews, for example, seem to have been more tolerated in Islamic Spain than in Christian Spain, and Buddhists living in Hindu areas have welcomed Islamic conquest in order to obtain a more tolerable status in society. But military aggression is a part of Islam, even if it is coupled with relative religious tolerance for non-Muslims. The jihad is a community obligation, which individuals can evade, but the flexibility of Muslim doctrine except for a few key points has allowed Islamic national rulers to utilize Islamic doctrine within political contexts for the purposes of defining and strengthening forms of nationalism.[19] Although Islam embraces a doctrine of just war, and requires that wars be defensive, Islamic scholars have had no greater difficulty than those in other traditions in locating particular excuses for particular military adventures.

Marxism has always presented itself as a revolutionary doctrine which entails the smashing of the capitalist system and its concomitant misery. At certain times, therefore, Marxism is theoretically the most bellicose religion we are considering, allowing scope for individual and collective revolutionary violence toward the end of inaugurating the classless society. Withdrawal from the world and anticipation of the afterlife are not comprehensible within Marxism, which focuses attention on the problem of achieving results in now time. Of course there are also humanist versions of Marxism which argue for reform rather than revolution and withdraw from killing wherever that is possible. In all versions, of course, the classless society itself is projected as without violence, since human nature and human ends would be in complete congruence there. In this way, Marxism shares in a pacifistic vision that can be found in all the major religious traditions under consideration.

A survey of the major religions on the issue of war reveals certain constancies in spite of variation in theology. All these religions contain the resources to marshal either pacifistic or bellicose versions in response to secular crisis, quite independently of the apparent major ideas within their systems. In all cases (except for that of Marxism applied to the revolutionary period) pacifistic versions seem only a step removed from central ideas. All the religions seem compelled to justify the notion of killing, and all have developed versions of the just-war doctrine, which at times seems blatantly contradictory, but is needed to bring the potentially critical thrust of religion into line with secular goals. Even the revolutionary activity of Marxism is justified ultimately by the final cessation of pain and suffering. Implicit in the just-war doctrine is the full critical potential of religion. Religions that have seen the world essentially as a battlefield (Zoroastrianism, dualist versions of Christianity such as Gnosticism) have not had staying power, perhaps because their critical stance vis-à-vis powerful modern states is compromised into bellicosity if the state becomes a rival power on the same spiritual level.

At the same time, the inability to stop war suggests that war may be intrinsic to civilization, and essentially to advanced civilization, and even suggests that war may have some covert but intrinsic relation to religion. Roger Callois has suggested that war is the only festival remaining for large civilizations. In smaller societies, the whole society could invert values for a period of religious renewal, perhaps in celebration and remembrance of the terrible original violence on whose continuing avoidance the society is now premised.[20] Our society is too complex for this. Only individuals can stop working for a time, as on Sunday in Christian societies, where essential services remain staffed by others. Religion inevitably becomes personalized in such a setting. War is the only remaining festival that can completely disrupt ordinary life for everyone. The individual becomes merged into the collectivity in a spasm of societal renewal. The constant, depressing threat of war may ultimately have some such basis, and this may explain in turn why the major religions seem compelled to stress a rational pacifism based on textual sources for ordinary comportment while being simultaneously fascinated and compelled by the possibility of war into developing an apparently contradictory doctrine of legitimate just war.

We shall now turn to the treatment of women in the various religious traditions, allowing this to stand also for associated problems between human beings within society.[21] As is the case with war, the actual treatment of women can vary quite independently of major textual claims, so that religious insight is often resolved with the actual status of women in families and society in a manner that seems curious to an outsider. Frequently, early stages of religion couple equality of humans before God with a relatively high status for women, which is leached away as the religion accommodates a surrounding patriarchal society. Second-class societal status for women is inevitably reflected, or so it seems, in second-class religious status. Frequently, civil law will borrow from religion in matters of family and sexual relationships, so that family law and religious law will be in coincidence, whereas civil law may largely ignore religious mandate in economic and political relationships primarily between men.[22] Women have had a special relationship to religion in nearly all the major traditions. Often shut out of the public spheres of economic and political competition, they have had to turn to religion to provide critical images that they could rely on in order to attempt to achieve their ends within the family context.[23] To some extent, this alliance may be forced upon women *in spite of* the content of the religion. The instrumental use of the body may be the only alternative tactical weapon, a fact that may explain the somewhat paradoxical simultaneous ascription of greater sensuality and spiritual sensitivity to women in various traditions. This would also help to explain why women's participation in religious institutions can be relatively high even though their official status is marginal within the religious hierarchy, even to the extent that they may be excluded from important posts because of their sex.

One of the strands woven into early Hinduism is worship of the phallus, a fact that can be intimated by the shape of many early religious figures. In the epics, the gods have a definite sexuality. They make love, they practice asceticism to gain strength, and they may tempt humans sexually. At the practical level, sex is discussed in terms of regulation and practice, and marital fidelity is frequently praised. At the same time, male needs are predominant, with the wife portrayed as subservient in the household, and educated courtesans available to men outside the home. Temple harlotry was a normal practice until British occupation sided with internal Hindu reform movements, and suppressed the practice. Dancing in the temple still occurs, but the erotic significance may be toned down, all the parts sometimes being danced by men. Courtship and sex are often discussed in essentially religious texts, as in the Kama Sutra. It should be noted that women have occupied the highest political offices in Hindu areas, and are able at least occasionally to overcome whatever secular and religious attitudes tell against their equality.

Tantric practices, a splinter of Hinduism, illustrate the pitfalls in any easy interpretation.[24] Tantric meditation is centered around the sex act, viewed as a way of achieving spiritual ecstasy and a feeling of mystical union. The universe is viewed as having monistic divine origins in a god who later assumes a bisexual form, the female form dancing the apparent complexity of the universe for the male form. Human intercourse is patterned after divine union. Mere physical contact is crude and repulsive; union must be based on meditation and spiritual preparation. Although Tantric practices are varied, and Tantric cults have been accused of orgies and license, in various legitimate forms preparation for union requires months, and the sex act itself is a lengthy affair demanding prolonged recitation and fondling. On this schedule of preparation, the sex act may occur only once a year. During union the relative passivity of the male may suggest feminine liberation to the unwary; the fact is that passivity is related to spiritual perfection and physical withdrawal, and the feminine role remains subservient.

Buddhism, particularly in the forms involving monks, represents an apparently more male-dominated religion, the sole founder being male. Sexuality is depressed in favor of the chastity that is related to enlightenment. Sexual relations threaten the vow of chastity and the search for detachment. There are female ascetics, who take similar vows to those enunciated by the monks, and who can be compared to nuns in the West, but their status is generally not as high as that of monks. The Buddha and other enlightened figures are frequently said to have been born of women who did not have sexual intercourse with men as a proximal cause of conception, and who died after giving birth before human sexual intercourse could be resumed. In lay matters, the Buddhist impact on caste, and the idea that salvation can be reached by everyone, permitted more freedom to women, without ensuring it. As in Hindu regions, women's social and political status may become quite high, as this is not the center of spiritual release.

Judaism deprecates celibacy, and priests and rabbis may marry. The play of sexual matters is not obscured in the texts, even to the embarrassment of later Christian commentators. The Song of Songs, for example, which apparently occupies a role analogous to that of erotic literature in Hinduism, is usually interpreted allegorically in Christianity. But at the heart of Judaic texts is the story of Adam and Eve, a story that permits Eve to be seen as having a derivative status in creation, and to be responsible for the fall and imperfect condition of human beings. Misogynistic interpretations of this sequence of events are frequent in historical Christianity, perhaps less frequent in Judaism. There remains, however, the impact of the Judaic view of the women as essentially existing inside a family, with lower civil status than males, as shown for example in courtroom proceedings.[25]

Christianity is the only religion to insist on monogamy from its inception, and to emphasize earthly love as a mere instrument for procreation. Jesus himself was an ascetic who was seemingly not married or ever sexually involved, and who carried the highest divine and separate standards of conduct through life. Love, for him, becomes in orthodox treatment a matter of *agape*, that is, a nonsexual spiritual caring to be sharply differentiated from *eros*. This allows the theoretical equality of women in the religion, in spite of the fact that Jesus himself was male, although note is taken that Jesus spoke freely to women. There is some evidence that the Trinity might originally have contained a feminine person, God the mother (Mary or Mary Magdalene), who could be addressed in prayer. Whatever feminine images may have existed, however, seem to have been rooted out in orthodoxy by the Pauline and Augustinian views.[26] Paul thought that women should keep their heads covered in church, and that they should remain silent. Augustine saw women as the source of sinful stimulation, and proposed that Christian husbands should hate their mortal wives to combat this, but love the creature of God within. As is well known, higher offices in orthodox churches have been closed to women.

Catholicism can lay claim to the status of Mary in order to argue the potentialities for spiritual equality, but it is an interesting exercise to consider various aspects of Mariolatry.[27] As much of orthodoxy seems to have been developed by men who feared women, Mary can be seen as a projective fantasy of a perfectly passive woman, without sin, a virgin whose passion and emotion is concentrated on caring for her God-child. Such a model may make real women look rather second class. Mary's very perfection can be a source of criticism of real women who are not like her. Nuns, as models of Mary in the real world, are expected to remain in quiet service roles. It is no wonder that the invocation of Mary does not by itself provide more than the basis for equality, no matter what the relationship of particular individuals to Mary in prayer. Further, there is no automatic basis for self-congratulation by Protestants. Although pastors may marry, and Protestantism does without celibate monks and nuns, women have had difficulty achieving higher hierarchical status, with the "pastor's wife" in reality an unbearably contradictory role. The transcendence of God leaves the pastor himself with little more to do than repeat ritual and provide lay counseling. On the whole, Christianity has the least to do overtly with sex and human passion, preferring to relegate it to the secular world where it can be discussed in novels, poetry, and the media.

Like Judaism and orthodox Christianity, Islam presents no duality based on sexual difference in the deity. The attachments of Islam, such as polygamy and the harem, have no doubt fueled orientalistic conjecture, and the facts of the Islamic treatment of women are complicated enough to lead to much divergence of opinion, inside and outside of Muslim culture. Muhammad, often portrayed as sensual because of his multiple marriages, seems better described as a modest man who frequently retired to the desert for meditation and prayer, and who married often for political reasons. The sexual energy with which he is credited may be part of the mythology of his popular appeal. In fact the Quran seems to have made women's status more equal than in prevailing society by limiting the number of wives so as to insure their more equal treatment in smaller groups and to see that unattached women were likely to find a place in a family, and by giving women control over their own dowries.[28] Early Islamic women seem to have had more freedom than Islamic women did later, as the adoption of the veil, which seems to predate Islam, and the adoption of other codes of women's conduct and seclusion brought about a permanent change in women's status. Women could no longer worship with men in mosques in spite of Muhammad's apparent instructions to the contrary. The veil may be seen as an advantage. As women had to go out frequently, and at night (no indoor sanitation being available), the veil can be seen as a protection against harassment of various kinds. Even in the home, the seclusion of women may be intended to prevent jealousy or comparison by visiting males. The veil and chador may also allow women to be treated more equally by distributing physical charm, and many Muslim women who have tried Western dress have preferred a return to Islamic tradition. Others, of course, have not. The veil may be seen as giving women second-class status, and as an attempt to prolong direct male control.[29] And there are those who find the veil seductive, an incitement rather than a deterrent to interest. All in all, the customs of Islam seem capable of benign or malignant use in the original setting of Islam, allowing reasonable protection of single women and permitting women to enter at least a largely independent society of their own, from which they may have felt free to criticize the patriarchal world around them. In modern settings, these customs are a barrier to integration with European society, a fact exploited differently by those who wish to further or to hinder this integration, showing once again that the resources of the religion may be exploited for secular purposes in quite different directions. Those on the fringes of modern civilization may cherish old ways as the only means of preventing a fall into the pit.[30]

This survey has been directed toward indicating that the resources of the major theological systems can typically be mobilized on various sides of important social issues. Where this has been noticed before, secular commentators have been tempted to find vacuity in the religious traditions, and religious commentators to trace preferred social postures from the relevant texts. I have been suggesting that this adaptability is a sign of the richness of the religious traditions, a sign of the fact that they provide the conceptual resources necessary to strike a critical stance against local injustices. At the same time, critique may attempt to legitimate what seems natural behavior. A set of detailed dogma put down once and for all would quickly grow stale, since it could not anticipate all the evolving features of human society. In any event, positions on social issues are sufficiently independent of theological resources so as to preclude any basis for evaluation of the religious traditions. They can be twisted into too many similar forms.

Where else can we look? There are some properties of the traditions that call out for explanation. For example, dance is almost absent in Christianity, dancing having been given over to the secular domain. Some movements of the priest or pastor can have aesthetic dimensions, but dance as an expression of life, as feeling the rhythm of the universe, seems cut off from the transcendent posture and cerebral nature of modern Christianity. Dancing is, simply put, too animal. God is too austere to enjoy dancing or the pleasure that dancers may feel in their dancing.[31] The universe is too orderly in principle to be conveniently represented in the complexity of dance movement. Dance gives us a feeling for one another, but the Christian service seems designed to still this impulse so that, even if individuality is muted, attention is directed heavenward. The absence of sacral dance is a much more pervasive aspect of Christian culture than any position that Christianity takes on social issues.[32] To understand the current status of Christianity, we need to look for clues like this which can be used to distinguish it from the other major traditions more surely than its abstract dogma can.

4

Grid, Group, and Religion

CHAPTER ANALYSIS   It may now seem that total confusion has been established. Suppose it granted that religion as critique is always possible, and that the major theologies can be articulated in support of specific social critique in an endless variety of ways. What is lacking now is any idea of how the traditions can be usefully distinguished if we have given up a comparative epistemological analysis, or what it is that may put constraints on the available theological resources at a given time. A slight acquaintance with history shows that religion's potential for critique seems dormant at certain points in history, and highly developed at other points. To complete an account of religion as critique, the next two chapters deal with the historical movement of Christianity from a confrontational stance against the state to its current position in which the theoretical potential of critique seems dormant. This analysis, while merely suggestive in terms of historical specificity, is intended to indicate how historical factors impinge on the theoretical possibility of critique.

The analysis, while it depends on the idea that theological structure can be asynchronous with surrounding society, depends also on the original Durkheimian insight that in a stable society religious and social structure may become isomorphic, with highly charged conceptual boundaries also in isomorphic relationships, allowing one to guess at social structure from religious prohibitions, and vice versa. Mary Douglas's analysis of the isomorphic possibilities is introduced, as well as her comparative analysis of structure based on the notions of *grid* and *group*. Specific versions of the major theological systems associated with specific societies may appear in various locations in the plane of comparative grid/group pressures, as well as in the conjectured societies proposed in utopian theology. It is suggested that societies in which no more than one pressure has been dominant can provide varying social critique, but need not experience religious change as opposed to the reinterpretation of an existing religion. Societies achieving high grid and high group, however, may experience conflicting pressures of high intensity that are resolved by a change in religious structure into separate grid and group religions. European Christianity, later exported to the United States, may have been the first of the major theological traditions to experience this splitting, with a church and state structure imposing partially conflicting religious demands turned into a split structure. Religious toleration, an essential step toward the modern state structure, still privileged certain connections to tradition. In the United States, the original association favored an even deeper split that became religious pluralism, and the divided demands of church and state offered the ideal soil for the growth of two different species of religion.

W<small>E</small> have been looking at the major religious traditions as providing the resources for critique of surrounding society, a critique that may be in the form of withdrawal from the society, or in the form of active criticism. Most of the major traditions clearly begin as critique, but they also show accommodating forms leading to doctrines that are congruent with surrounding secular attitudes, especially where the traditions have been historically successful in shaping that society. Any effort to understand the current religious situation seems fatally compromised by this confusion of forms. Aspects of pure theological roots can be distinguished, but these grow into quite different and overlapping foliage in secular soil. We expect major traditions to show divergent forms that cannot all be legitimating for surrounding society, cannot simply reflect surrounding society, but will take on the form of surrounding society in that permission and prohibition will obviously be related to societally given possibilities.

If Christianity is our primary concern, we can return to the independence of domain granted to Christianity and science. Socially accommodated forms of Christianity seem optional, matters for personal decision, even though we have argued that religion in general is not decisional, but consists of values that seem forced onto one's actions as central sources of critique. If we can't read up from secular scientific knowledge to verify or falsify religious claims, what can be relevant to establishing the legitimacy of religious values in Western society? Sociologists have often looked to religion as legitimating basic social values; but where religion can take on conflicting forms, this supposition confronts serious problems. A conflicted society could reflect divergent religions, but this tempts an analysis of society as a collection of subsocieties. If we retain the basic intuition that modern nations can be viewed as societies for sociological purposes, there are other possibilities. One possibility is that modern societies reflect partially or wholly unnoticed religions that are not necessarily identical to the religious traditions represented institutionally in them. In this case, the religion of the society is an instance of the sociological generalization about society and religion, while the institutionally preserved traditions provide resources for support or critique of societal values reflected into the societal religion. The potential of critique preserved in tradition is what interests us here as a continuance of the original power of religious insight, and as a purchase of distance on surrounding society when its means of presenting itself become consolidated in pervasive communications media. For Christianity, then, there is the possibility that coercive Christian values can be used in critique of surrounding society, and that the contemporary interest in Christianity must lie in this fact, rather than in sociological indicators of the secularization of Christian institutions.

Human beings do not encounter a purely natural world, they encounter a world that is a cultural object in the sense that culture determines what is significant in the world, and how significant objects should be treated. Part of culture is language, and part of it is religion. It is clear that neither language nor religion can simply reflect society, if only because the weight of tradition embodied in these cultural components must typically lag behind current social structure, especially in the case of successful religions. The gap between tradition and current structure may be a source of progressive critique as well as conservative hysteresis. Tradition can become critique only when it is not a reflection, so that critique can appear in the gaps between traditional ideas and present reality.[1]

Societies that do not change much over time may develop a religion that is reflective of social structure, and it is of course these kinds of societies that were the focus of Durkheim's analysis of religion as reflected social structure.[2] If religion does have an intimate connection with social structure because of its status in culture, no particular causality is implied. Social structure *and* religion may be the result of transcendent entrance into human society, or religion could be merely a vast reflection of society (or past society) through language and culture. The reflective approach can tell us nothing about the transcendent status of religion, but it can help us to discern the outline of religious conviction.

In what follows, I shall attempt to utilize the reflective approach to discern the status of religion without implication for its cognitive claims of transcendence. But I will bear in mind that the societies I will be principally observing are not static, but are changing rapidly. This permits the situation where religious systems of belief are likely to be out of synchronization with attitudes in surrounding society, so that they can provide critical potential. At the same time, society will still have a structure that can be reflected in consciousness and in religion, a structure that may diverge from the structure represented in official religions. We should be prepared to discover, for example, that the religion of official Christianity, while it may provide the resources for a critique of current society, is somewhat at odds with the imposed values of current society. But these are anticipatory speculations. We need a way to find reflected structure if we are to do any investigation.

For the rest of our discussion, I will utilize ideas that have been worked out by Mary Douglas in developing a framework for comparing forms of social control that has its roots in Durkheim's theory of reflection.[3] In order to grasp how this works, we will look at one of Mary Douglas's most convincing analyses, her analysis of the Abominations of Leviticus.[4] The significance of this example is related to the fact that food selection and preparation in society is always a component of culture.[5] What can be eaten and how it may be prepared seem subject to the sort of imposed cultural values that we have associated with religious belief. Almost anything may be eaten in one part of the world, and prohibited with conviction (and perhaps revulsion) elsewhere. American abhorrence of horse meat as food for humans is sufficient to indicate that this phenomenon is not subject entirely to explanation in terms of health hazard or nutritional theory, but has also a definite cultural determinant.

At first sight, the Judaic prohibitions seem arbitrary and odd. They have been subjected to attempts at explanation that center around various seemingly rational possibilities. Some have accepted the rules as arbitrary, and have argued that the Jewish priests were attempting to set an artificial boundary around the society that they were attempting to control. Or perhaps the prohibitions were not arbitrary, but were chosen to separate the Jews from surrounding cultures. Anthropological research indicates that the Jews were not unique in their food customs, and the plausibility that a binding and lasting religion can be constructed consciously by scheming priests seems small. We can set these efforts aside as not providing any very satisfactory insight. Others have suggested that Moses simply picked the most nutritious meats and foods, but this suggestion encounters several difficulties. What is nutritious seems determined by culture partly, and not by the natural state of the world. Further, it can't be argued that the pig is not nutritious, so a special case needs to be made here. The diseases that the pig threatens could have been controlled by proper cooking, and it seems gratuitous to argue that the pig is so delicious that it was forbidden in an effort to control gluttony. There is the possibility that the pig was associated with an alien style of life, and we will return to this shortly. There is also an allegorical or symbolic interpretation. References to the divided hoof and chewing of the cud can be interpreted as signs of the difference between good and evil or of the value of meditation. But in the absence of a system of natural signs, this sort of interpretation could be forced onto almost any set of food prohibitions, turning them into a reflection of Christianity.

Mary Douglas's solution to the details of the prohibitions was to trace them back to concepts indigenous to the Hebrew language. The culture is here being defined, but in a language that had been relatively unchanging. Concepts expressed in the language have certain natural borders, and certain paradigmatic exemplars. The completeness or purity of objects was related to centrality in conceptual groupings. Living animate creatures were divided into creatures of the water, creatures of the air, and creatures of the land. Associated with each kind is a preferred, or normal mode of moving about associated with paradigm creatures. Within each group, central creatures were fit for the table, and the most perfect examples of the air and land varieties were fit for the altar (all of this after correct preparation). Creatures sharing some but not all the criteria for normality were then assessed according to their overlap with normality. For example, among creatures of the air, flying or hopping is the normal means of movement, and these creatures are expected to have wings and two legs. Creatures of the air failing these criteria are not edible. In all groups, swarming creatures are abominable, presumably because swarming was viewed as a mysterious and unnatural means of locomotion, a movement with no clearly distinguishable parts, and no clear leader or organization. Hopping locusts, by comparison, are edible. Among creatures of the land, cloven-hoofed, cud-chewing ungulates are the proper food for pastoralists, given by God. Wild game are not complete by comparison, and can only be eaten if they conform as closely as possible to paradigm examples of ungulates.

This conceptual framework and its related theoretical approach solve very neatly the organization of the abominations, as a comparison of Douglas's treatment to the texts will indicate. Further, her original account can be strengthened by other considerations.[6] There is evidence to suggest that plants were originally the proper food for man, with animals only an occasion for sacrifice to God, as only God could properly take the soullike aspects of animals in sacrifice. Man's corruption (the Garden of Eden, the Flood) leads to man's eating meat as a recognition of man's evil.[7] But meat must be specially prepared by removing its blood. Blood is the divine aspect that must be removed if meat is a properly desacralized food for man. The priest, in letting the blood of a murdered animal, expiates the murder through sacrifice. An elaborate code of clean versus unclean food is put into the dietary laws. Carnivorous animals also break the conceptual framework in that animals should eat plants, and not animals.[8] Carnivores with clawed feet, or animals that can be carnivorous (pigs) are forbidden food, but ruminants are not, since their digestive apparatus and feeding habits are strictly vegetarian. Cloven-hoofed animals are problematic in this respect, as domestic ruminants are cloven-hoofed but the horse and the ass are not.

What is clean and holy must be without blemish, and in a natural state. Unleavened, salted bread preserves the original state of the flour, whereas fermentation alters the nature of flour. Further, the idea that things have natural properties that should not be mixed is reflected elsewhere in Judaic codes. Crossbreeding is prohibited, as is the yoking together of an ox and an ass. Planting should be done with only one kind of seed, and one should wear only one form of cloth at a time.[9] Clothes should be appropriate to one's sex, as should one's sexual activities.[10] Even such prohibitions as that a kid should not be boiled in its mother's milk can be read as an extension of the general rule that a mother and her son must keep separate lives, i.e., as a symbolic prohibition of incest.[11] The sanctity of God, the idea that he cannot be confused with other gods or idols without disaster, is an integral part of this scheme.

This approach through structural considerations is powerful, and it leads to substantial insights where religion and culture are temporally congruent, as in our test case. But it won't solve all our problems.[12] For one thing, it is simply not the case that all cultures condemn as abominable what doesn't fit their categories. Second, the structural approach doesn't explain the particular abhorrence of the pig. It may reflect historical factors, but it can't explain their differential intensity. The first question may have a relatively simple answer based on the exclusivity of Judaic culture. The Jews were not interested in intermarriage or in cultural exchange. Fear of cultural exchange may be related to the fear of classificatory anomalies. Where a cultural group cannot be self-sufficient, and must trade and exchange with other cultures, conceptual border anomalies may be seen as benign.[13] Thus the fear of anomaly may be related to a specific type of culture which the Jews represented.

The reason for special abhorrence of swine flesh has engendered bitter controversy. It is possible to single out some quasi-structural aspects of the pig that may be relevant. The pig is different because, if kept as a domestic animal, it is raised just for food, whereas cows and other domestic food animals play other roles supportive of the human economy before they are killed for food. The cow may seem a paradigm domestic helper, because it can provide milk, butter, and cheese and seems divinely designed for domesticity. Pigs, raised just to be eaten, may seem unnaturally domesticated by comparison. But, of course, this would place no barrier to eating wild swine flesh. According to Jewish dietary laws, blood must be drained from meat that is to be eaten at the table. The pig, by eating carrion and who knows what, prospers in apparent violation of the principles of the dietary laws, and presents problems in proper preparation, since one cannot know what the pig contains. So, even if domesticated, the pig is a wild animal and not proper food. Is this sufficient to locate the pig's special place in dietary considerations?

A negative answer has been given by authors who wish to reject the notion that culture is an autonomous or semiautonomous variable determining what nature is, and what it contains, for human beings in a specific society. Such authors may argue that there is always a rational explanation for what seem odd cultural practices, an approach involving explanation in terms of immediate advantage for the individuals in the relevant society. Marvin Harris has been an exponent of such an approach.[14] Harris can agree with Douglas that medical materialism is nonsense, and that the pig was not banned because of someone's awareness of trichinosis and its dangers. Harris argues that the pig is integral to the manner of life of some societies contemporary with Jewish society at the time in question, and that the abhorrence of the pig is simply an expression of fear that the cultivation of pigs would alter the entire Jewish way of life. As nomadic pastoralists, they lived in unforested hilly plains whose grassy areas provided the food for the cattle, sheep, and goats that were at the heart of their economies. These pastoralists maintained contact with the farmers who were stationary around oases and rivers. The pig is indigenous to the forests and shady riverbanks of the farmers, and cannot be herded long distances to the schedule of the pastoralist. It should stay close to water for purposes of temperature control, a fact also limiting movement.[15] On Harris's view, the succulent nature of cooked pork was a threat to the Jewish life style, a threat combated by Jewish priests with a consequently focused resistance.

Harris's general approach has been subjected to severe and damaging criticism. To begin with, Harris relies on a general explanatory framework for societies that involves their attempts to maximize protein intake. This notion is dubious on nutritional grounds, and may well be a projection of American dietary preferences onto other cultures.[16] Further, Harris's approach loses much of its explanatory power in the case of Islamic pig prohibition, where the prohibition may have evolved to protect a centralized political hierarchy and prevent the formation of autonomous pockets of Islamic power.[17] But these technical aspects of Harris's general program do not concern us here. The problem with Harris's program is its limited scope. No matter how well it may apply to pig prohibition in this one context, it cannot begin to explain the full scope of dietary abomination. Why are things that are not nearby evaluated in the Judaic code, such as creatures of the ocean? On Douglas's view, the whole universe is mirrored in the dietary laws, because they reflect the total set of concepts in which the universe is interpreted. The general outlines of purity and danger seem to be best explained by Douglas's cultural approach, although we can append Harris's considerations in a specifically historical form to explain why the pig is a special double polluter, representing an important conceptual anomaly and a threat to the Jewish way of life. In what follows, we shall assume the potential power of Douglas's approach, and see how far it will take us in an analysis of the current religious situation.

The approach we are considering holds that we order our environment through contrasts that are coded into names. Anything that threatens this system is potentially polluting and dangerous. It might seem that this basic idea is appropriate to various primitive cultures, but not to our own, since we now have separated religion from science and from hygiene within the sphere of culture. We shall hold to the contrary, that magic and religion remain integral parts of our culture, but that the problem is to locate such phenomena. We don't see the symbolic system that orders our world; rather we experience the world through that system. When one uses a tool for a long enough time, one may work through the tool and experience reality directly through it, without being aware of the tool. Culture is the means by which we experience reality, and we don't really notice it until it fails to work in some anticipated way. We see others as utilizing culture and symbols because they do not react the same way that we do to certain situations. What we notice is the difference between their way and our way, and that difference becomes the measure of arbitrary symbolism in their interaction with the world, while our use of culture remains tacit as the standard of measurement. How can we obtain clues to our cultural interaction with the world? An obvious way would be to internalize another culture, and then "look back" at the original, as people often do in some sense when they convert to a major religion. Short of this, and no method can insure the success of such internalization, we must employ much more indirect means.

Let us begin by noticing that the Abominations of Leviticus bear certain resemblances to our own dietary assumptions. As do the abominations, we tend to divide potential edible creatures into creatures of the water (fish), creatures of the land (animals), and creatures of the air (birds).[18] Border creatures, insects and reptiles, are generally not regarded as edible.[19] Edible water creatures are centrally freely moving fish with scales, and so forth, and except for certain gourmets, people seem repulsed by the idea of eating eels and other marginal creatures. Among the animals, the very close (domestic pets) and the very remote (zoo animals) are not regarded as edible. Livestock may be eaten when properly killed and prepared. The existence of poachers, for example, is an oddity that leaves unaffected reluctance in the general population to eat game except under special circumstances. Birds and beasts are perceived as being like humans in some ways, for example there are human versions of these creatures in children's stories, and edible examples must be humanely killed by our cultural standards. The distant lobster, on the other hand, can be boiled alive. A study of these divisions shows that they are not so remote from the abominations we started with, probably because of obvious cultural roots.

The perceived closeness of animals to human beings has some interesting linguistic accompaniments. Familiar animals have short names that can also be applied to human beings; for example, *bitch, cat, pig, swine, ass, goat,* and *cur* are recognizable insults, while *lamb* and *duck* are sometimes used affectionately. Distance is increased by the use of special names for animals; *Lassie, Rex,* and *Benji.* Where edibility comes into question, special names are utilized to screen the natural origins. Edible parts of a cow and pig that bear anatomical resemblance to human muscle are relabeled *roast, steak, chops,* and *chuck,* while the relatively inedible innards remain the heart, kidney, and tongue. Our meals are centered around these permissible meat dishes, steak remaining expensive and prestigious in spite of the relative scarcity of the entirely edible tongue. This should be sufficient to indicate the cultural component of our eating restrictions. At the border, and this is important for what happens later, anxiety may surface. We can conceive of eating horse meat, and in fact our pet dogs may do so, but can our pet dogs be eaten? If not, it is not because they are not edible, as experience with cultures where dogs are eaten will indicate. Viewed from such a culture, incidentally, our own seems to have, in fact, its own sacred animals.

The discharges of the human body are universally the objects of taboo, in particular, feces, urine, semen, nasal discharges, menstrual blood, hair clippings, nail parings, spit, and even sweat. This seems reasonably explained by the problems of personal boundary. Are these things part of the person who had eliminated them, or not? Because of their ambiguity, they are the objects of manipulation in various forms of malevolent magic. Perhaps our culture has transcended these problems. Or has it? Certain names for these objects are not regularly permitted as part of polite, or public, discourse, and broaching related subject matter may prove socially awkward. Consider this riddle: "What does a rich man carefully put into his pocket that a poor man throws away?"[20] An answer, of course, is *snot*; but the uneasiness that an attempt to discuss the social significance of this riddle can bring is often marked even in supposed liberal academic circles.[21] Relaxation or disappearance of excretory anxieties in our culture may be due to such simple matters as our plumbing and waste systems, which mix up our waste so thoroughly with other substances that it cannot be identified for purposes of malevolent magic. But let us look at some other matters. We will drink water from a glass, and swallow our own spit, without thought. But many find it disgusting to drink from a glass of water into which they have spit. Now let us look at the slightly more complicated matter of aversion to those who have a common cold.[22] Medically, the chances of catching a cold from a person with manifest symptoms seem to be marginal, although this is given by both parties as the excuse for avoiding meetings when someone has the relevant symptoms. Could it be that a person with a cold makes us queasy because the normal borders of the person become indeterminate during a cold? What are the boundaries of someone who has sneezed? What is the extent of a cough or a sneeze associated with a cold? We may be made relatively queasy by cancer, as opposed to other serious diseases. Again, this may be because cancer and its means of transmission are simply not understood as, for instance, a heart attack is, and therefore has indeterminate boundaries. The problems and taboos associated with personal boundary may shift, rather than disappear, in a society with indoor plumbing and modern science. This is the possibility that will be relevant to religion as well.

We are interested in locating some classificatory trends more specific to various societies, more indicative of their differences, than some of the space-time categories that are common to many cultures. If religion is to be read as reflective of categorical schemes, the level of abstraction must be kept low enough to permit the discovery of religious differences. Two major spatial axes have been noted in diverse cultures with a similar valorization: right, as opposed to left, and higher, as opposed to lower.[23] In known cases, except for explicit deviance, the former of each couple is associated with high value. Not all evaluations need conform to these symbolic systems, as in the case of knowledge, where *deep* or *basic* may have positive connotations, but in cultural relationships of human power these symbolic systems tend to be predominant. The higher parts of the body (erect posture) tend to be sacred, and the lower, profane, and homage may be paid to superiors by lowering oneself before them. A chair or throne may elevate one permitted to sit on it, of course, a fact requiring adjustment in any crude version of vertical classification.[24] In any event, we must find a more sophisticated analysis of human relations if we are to locate religious differentiation.

Let us now turn to Mary Douglas's notions of *grid* and *group*.[25] As conceived by Douglas, these represent two forms of social control of the individual which the individual may negotiate by means of various strategies. In her own writing, she prefers to speak of individuals as though they could stand over and against these forms of control, in order (partially) to explain societal change. The method of grid and group is designed to contrast two forms of social control that an individual might feel. My treatment, although heavily indebted to Douglas, is not coincident with any of her published treatments, or with those by other authors.[26] In fact, there is a divergence between various treatments of these concepts by various authors, as they are put to different uses in different contexts. None of the extant treatments is designed to deal with contemporary comparative religion, and I have modified the concepts toward this end.

We are interested in a two-dimensional structure whose abscissa and ordinate we will call *group* and *grid*. It will not be possible to do more than order the group or grid pressure on individuals. We will organize the discussion of the relationship of grid and group with respect to a box divided into four smaller boxes as follows:

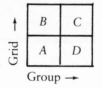

The function of the subdivision of the box is to enable us to compare four different situations, low grid *and* low group pressure (*A*), low grid but strong group pressure (*D*), strong grid but low group pressure (*B*), and strong grid *and* strong group pressure (*C*). Since only comparative, rather than quantitative, differences can be discussed, this scheme will enable us to make some useful comments about the cases that will prove important for comparing religious traditions. Let us begin by comparing *B* and *D*, that is, the situations where either grid or group pressure is strong and the other pressure is low. With constant low grid pressure, increasing group pressure means that the individual human being will recognize an increasingly strong border between members of the group defining group pressure and outsiders, people who do not belong to the group. The behavior of people *within* the group will be normatively constrained by group standards and expectations. These standards and expectations need not be articulated. They may be implicit in shared experiences. Possibilities for individual decision and action are swamped by identification with the others and the pressure of their expectations. Deviancy may be met with the sanction of expulsion. Within a strong group, what is right is likely to be nearly obvious, and sharply distinguished from what prevails outside the group. Because of the strong border, the outside will be a matter of mystery to which will be attached very strong negative valorizations. A member of a strong group need not be conceived of as an individual who has decided to join the group. The individual may pursue an individual life without reflection on the differences between an autonomous person and the constraints of group expectations. Communication within a strong group at low grid may be largely in a restricted code, which means that language will be understood between people without extensive elaboration of its meaning.[27] Past context associated with language will be important to its understanding. Communication, in short, will not require the sort of search for mutual intelligibility required when strangers are attempting to find common ground. Group membership will provide the common ground. Many small human groups may have existed in the situation described by *D*, with tradition providing at least part of the source of group expectations. In particular, the originating groups in Judaism, Christianity, Islam, and Marxism have shown some of these characteristics before the elaboration of a graded social hierarchy in larger populations. The psychological feel of control may be observed in close-knit groups of teenagers, who may rigorously conform to group expectation in the matter of fads and fashions of obscure origin. It may be difficult for them to articulate the origins or even the significance of their codes to outsiders while feeling very definitely the necessity of sending the right messages. Restricted strong group control may only be associated with groups small enough for the members to recognize one another, a reason why this form of pressure becomes inevitably mingled with grid control as population increases.

With constant low group pressure, on the other hand, increasing grid pressure means that the human being finds him- or herself a participant in a concrete social network whose articulated position involves the performance of circumscribed duties and expectations. Grid involves a structure and a place within that structure. Associated with the place is a set of expectations. These expectations are not given by the inarticulate expectations of others which may shift in an unanticipated way over time, rather these expectations will be set out in an elaborated code that attaches the expectations to the proper places in the grid. In fact, individuals are insulated from feeling one another's expectations by the very rigidity of performance attached to the code of expectations. Each is able, in theory, to perform according to code expectations quite isolated from the way in which other persons at other locations are performing. It may be, of course, that power flows through the grid in such a fashion that persons at some locations must accept orders or requests from persons at other locations, at least certain kinds of orders or requests that are specified by the appropriate rules of the grid. An army private in our society seems caught in such a grid, as are the occupants of other military ranks. The duties and expectations attached to these posts are set out in careful rules, and their performance is insulated as much as possible from personality or negotiation. There is a heavy sanction attached to failure to follow the expectations attached to the place in the structure. Outside of this fact, one's personal characteristics are largely irrelevant to grid evaluation. Historically, societies with caste distinctions provide an example of societies with obvious grid expectations.

Grid and group are logically compatible. A society with a strong group border could also have an elaborated grid within that border, and the pressure on individuals might be nicely separated into compatible grid and group expectations. At the same time, simultaneous grid and group pressures might not be compatible, causing severe problems of personal adaptation. This situation will prove to be very important to our investigation, although it has not assumed a large role in previous grid/group analyses of social structure. Where both grid and group are weak, external pressure is obviously minimized, allowing the possibility that members of some kind of human collective will have to constantly negotiate their relative status and mutual expectations. This situation will not prove important for our investigation, but it completes a preliminary logical sorting of the conceptual possibilities.

Any general comparative discussion of grid and group in societies runs into the tremendous problems of social difference. To explain the notions more clearly, however, we can suppose that the populations of two societies are identical in size, and that there are no important structural differences between the societies except those introduced by the notions of grid and group structure. The strength of the border that defines whether a person belongs inside or outside the society is then a measure of group strength. As the border becomes stronger, it becomes clearer and clearer just who is linked to any member of the society in a network of mutual expectational pressure. Societies can be represented as circles whose circumferences become heavier and heavier as they shift toward high group to indicate the strength of this border. Under the same simplifications, the sheer number of differentiated social roles functions as a measure of grid, so that grid can be represented by a number of labels for these roles inside the circle, the number representing how many such roles there are, and the number increasing as the circles representing societies shift toward high grid.

Now grid roles carry their own specifications for expected behavior, so that social pressure is represented at a grid role by a traditional specification of role expectations. Toward the left-hand
vertical border, these specifications would tend to be detailed and
complete. As a circle moved to the right, the same number of social
roles could become less well defined, and more freedom for the
holder of the role to determine his or her own behavior in the role
could make itself evident, until it was replaced by group constraints, and finally total group control. This movement could be
represented by a gradual lightening of the role labels in the circle
until at the right-hand vertical border they would disappear, no
matter how many of them there were. Obviously, the strength of
the circumference of the circle would be inversely correlated to the
strength of the role markers under these circumstances, introducing
a redundancy into the representation corresponding to the relationship between grid and group that we wish to assert. Could we find
the right societies, these differences could be operationalized and
assigned a representation. One might be able to determine the number of nouns for social positions in the languages involved as a measure of grid, for example, and perhaps find a convincing measure of
group in something like the strength of terms of disapprobation
that can be analytically linked to nonmembership in the group, or
a measure of the difficulty one encounters in becoming a member of
the group.

Whatever plausible measures might be found for this idealized
case, almost any real situation initially presents seemingly over-
whelming difficulties. But, as elsewhere in theorizing, complexity
needs to be broken into manageable aspects. For example, the
number of roles may have to be relativized to the size of the population if an effective measure of grid is to be located. One might
expect that greater differentiation of roles is necessary or likely for
social administration in a larger society, and the grid dimension
would need to reflect this fact. An even more complex problem is
that of social institutions. We may need to compare societies in
which there is basically only one internal institution that is highly
differentiated with societies where there are a variety of institutions

each of which is less highly differentiated. In other words, we may need to consider how the members of the society are distributed among the social roles. When the societies could be represented as circles, this was because all the social positions could be located roughly at the same grid/group mix. When societies have to be analyzed into subsystems, any convenient comparative judgment may be lost. Various subsystems may require placement at different points of the grid/group plane, or the society may have to be broken down completely into different individual placements. Further, members of a highly differentiated society may respond to different grid/group pressures in different roles, for example roles they assume at work or in the home. In short, grid/group doesn't solve the problems of sociology, it simply provides a measure to represent them that is suggestive from the standpoint of the study of religion. Perhaps this will be sufficient to indicate that the notions can be given empirical content. We are interested here only in utilizing these notions to make a relatively crude historical placement of Christianity, and these parameters seem sufficient to motivate the possibility of the historical development that concerns us.

Whenever one moves off the sides of the box defining zero group or zero grid, one is subject to two different forms of social control, and this will be the normal situation. Further, it is possible to imagine a society whose members are largely in *D* that establishes a set of hierarchical codified practices which represents a fixed tradition that can come to exert grid control on later members of the same society. In a sense, the society can be said to move from *D* to *B* over time. We will assume here that at the upper-left corner and the lower-right corner of the box the pressures are consistent, or at least that one consistent form of pressure is dominant. A person could live in a society with contradictory grid pressure, or contradictory group pressure, but we will assume that a person will see him- or herself primarily as a member of at least one consistent subgroup of the society in such circumstances, adjusting predominant pressure to the detail of situation. It would be hard to imagine how a person perceiving sharply contradictory pressures could stay functional for very long without compartmentalization, so our simplifying assumption seems at least true to the pressures a person is likely to consciously accept as impinging on him or her in a particular situation.

Individuality or ego in any self-assertive sense seems nonexistent or minimal at the corners mentioned, and perhaps we can assume that the diagonal connecting the other two corners is where we are likely to locate strong self-assertive notions of human individuality. Let us call this the ego line:

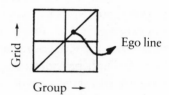

At the lower-left end, grid and group are weak, so we may expect people in *A* to be individuals who are constantly struggling and negotiating directly with other members of their society for short-term advantages and mutually tolerable relationships. Long-term change cannot be stabilized by grid or group structural pressure. For action to occur here, individuality will have to elevate itself, since direction is not supplied by grid or by group. In C, however, a different situation obtains. Here grid and group both exert strong pressure. But individuality may be necessary to sort out the pressures of grid and group, which at least theoretically may conflict strongly. This possibility will prove fundamental to our later considerations. As an interim example, however, let us consider a teenager or factory worker who is caught in a situation where group loyalties are in conflict with the grid policies of some bureaucracy within which the group is embedded, and which has powers of control over the group. A particular individual may filter out one form of pressure to achieve resolution, but a person sensitive to both pressures may need to resolve the situation through application of a highly abstract and detailed set of moral rules. Therefore a strong sense of individuality may be present all along the ego line.

When we move below the ego line, group pressure predominates over grid pressure. The autonomous individual has an identity that gets bound up with that of others. There is mutual feeling, mutual responsibility, mutual accommodation. Boundaries widen to include other members of the group integrally into one's concerns and plans of action. Ego is retained, but the individual no longer calculates only to his or her personal advantage. As we move above the ego line, grid pressure predominates over group pressure. The autonomous individual becomes increasingly controlled by an apparently impartial system. Individuality needs only to function well enough to recognize one's position and the attendant duties. When we reach the left side of the diagram, the ego has shrunk to the null point, and when we reach the bottom side, ego has expanded its boundaries to the limits of society. Above the line, the real universe is less important than the rules of the grid, but below the line the group (in the world) becomes the focal point of attention.

Now we have to deal with what we are putting into the graph. Since the graph is a measure of felt social control, individuals who feel this control could be represented in various orderings in terms of the felt intensity of group and grid. There are a variety of problems that render the grid/group graph ultimately problematic. We don't have a good way of measuring felt intensity of control between individuals, or across cultures. Further, one person in a given society may feel quite different grid and group pressures as he or she moves from situation to situation, feeling less control (or more) inside the family, for example, than on the job.[28] It won't be our purpose here to develop the complicated techniques for measuring felt control (or even control) that would be required to complete a scientific use of this conceptual device. Our purpose will be to use it in a subjective way to discuss some comparisons in religious systems. As we have noted, the religions themselves take on such varied forms, particularly in local contexts, that some adherents of the major religions in some social setting will almost certainly be locatable in each of the four boxes. We will therefore have to project some hypothetical ideal types based on the consideration of the major traditions that we have undertaken if we are to use grid/ group analysis to make some comparisons.

Before we do this, we need to look also at the gap between an ideal, conjectured social relationship and the secular pressures actually felt by individuals. Common to Judaism, Christianity, Islam, and Marxism, for example, and quite independent of other features of these religions, is a vision of happy human beings living in a collective where everyone cares about, and shares with, the other members of the collective. Particular sect members may feel that they have achieved, or partially achieved, this status within the larger secular society where they live. Should we compare idealized situations or actual, typical secular positions? Here we will opt for the latter, and consider the actual situations of religious adherents in typical secular settings, accepting as a temporary given the association of accommodated institutional religions with the values of surrounding secular states.

When grid/group analysis confronts anthropological data, smaller traditional societies are scattered about *A* and *D*, and appear to some extent also in *B*. The reasons for this tend to be consequences of the pressures we are considering. A low grid, high group society will have little internal specialization, and individual relationships will be ambiguous. Internal conflict can be resolved by expulsion of bad actors, or fission, so the cost of public conflict can be high. Disagreement is driven underground, and ill will and frustration will be below the surface. This type of society tends to remain small. Fission will occur when it gets large, and there is not enough grid structure to support administration of a large society through specialized roles. In *A*, there can be high competition, with rewards going to innovators or lucky individuals who succeed in manipulating others for their own advantage. Fall from high status may come quickly. There will be attention to success in the short run, for this reason. Again, the lack of grid limits stability and size, since division of labor and control of society is difficult without grid traditions.

High grid is compatible with small societies, but it can sustain larger societies. The power maintaining the constraining relationships is remote and impersonal, so that stability can be sanctioned if the power continues to hold, and a complex society can function if the code of the grid permits successful accommodation to the situations that actually present themselves. A combination of high grid and high group allows flexibility where change can be brought about by group action, which is then transmitted in changes to the social structure. One might expect large, complex technological societies to cluster, consequently, in C.

Now let us turn to some variables that may seem more directly associated with religion and social structure. Let us consider shame, guilt, sin, and evil. Can we, to begin with, distinguish shame and guilt?[29] Shame and guilt have been distinguished in a variety of ways. Public humiliation, and an audience, are required for shame, even if shame may be felt in anticipation of public exposure. Shame is indicative of failure against the criterion of a public model or a publicly ascribed expectation. A person who is shamed may want privacy, and may wish to retreat from public view. Shame itself is exposure before the relevant public, if only in the imagination. Where there are public rules of conduct, or expected codes of conduct associated with positions within a hierarchy, shame is the result of their objective violation. In this sense, shame can be anticipated if a violation is likely. Shame can be transported to others. We can feel ashamed for others, particularly when their shameful violations are related to our own social status. Guilt, on the other hand, occurs when a private standard is violated, or when a private or nonarticulated expectation is not satisfied. Guilt need not have a public manifestation, no matter how intensely it is felt. We make a promise, and fail to keep it. Guilt can result. The promise may be made to others, or to oneself, as when one adopts a private rule of conduct that one then violates. In this sense, guilt cannot be anticipated. It may be felt when one decides or feels that the agreement was broken without justification. Guilt may seek exposure and punishment without which it cannot be expiated. From this point of view, shame is self-sufficient, and perhaps can be eradicated, but guilt can be terminated by compensatory exposure and punishment. What is sometimes called guilt may be considered rather guilty fear, as when one violates a public code, feels apprehension, but is relieved when not apprehended. The difference here is that the violated code need not be a personal commitment. These brief remarks suggest that shame may be predominant in B and C, high grid areas, where positional attainments will have attached standards of conduct. Guilt may be predominant in C and D where the absence of hierarchy forces private agreements and private standards, many of them not fully articulable. In the Old Testament, Adam and Eve may feel shame when they recognize their nakedness, but the covenantal agreement between the Jews and their God inevitably introduces a dominant theme of guilt and expiation into violations of the code. We are speaking then of dominant patterns that will become very complicated as the ego line is approached. In the upper ego-line area, for example, simplified codes of behavior related to social position, allowing a certain exploration in behavior to social positions, can give rise to complicated patterns of guilt and shame. In A, on the other hand, it would seem that both guilt and shame are inappropriate and setbacks merely the result of stupidity or bad planning, and an occasion to vow to try harder next time.

Sin is the breaking of rules of conduct legislated directly by divine sources. As rules and associated pressure are at a minimum in A, the concept of sin will be scarce here. In $B, C,$ and D, sin can be coupled with guilt or shame, depending on the local circumstances; but a difference in redemption will be associated with the particular circumstances. Sin that is the result of grid violation may be redeemed by public ritual or public punishment. Sin that is the result of group violation may be difficult to expunge, since it depends on an inner change. Expulsion may come anyway because of the ambiguities of public life. In some classical versions of Christianity, sin means expulsion from grace, where only God is able to see whether the sin has been followed by true repentence, and only God can forgive sin on the basis of this repentence. Evil seems to involve sin that is accomplished knowingly and perhaps in a premeditated fashion. We can expect to find evil in C on the ego line because of this basis in individual action. But below the ego line in C and D, evil may persist when one knowingly does something that causes harm to others, or involves them in harm, and does not expiate the act. The interpenetration of ego here means that the evil person can cause ill to others by association in the absence of expiation, so the effort to cure or expel may be frantic. Unfortunately, where there are no clear guidelines for expiation in the absence of a grid structure sufficient to detail the expiating act, the consequences of evil are literally incalculable, and may foment unfocused hostility and suspicion. In all areas of the grid/group graph, of course, there will be bad people, people who are evaluated negatively for what they have done, or what they have attempted. We have been looking only at the more characteristically religious aspects of human failure.

In areas *A, B,* and *D,* one may expect the relatively low levels of grid or group control to be associated with fairly undifferentiated domains of the sacred and the profane. The distinction will be drawn, but it will invade nearly all aspects of everyday life. Where a sharply distinct group and grid pressure is possible, in the upper right-hand quadrant *C,* we might theorize the possibility that the sacred and the profane could be separated in terms of control, one associated with grid control, and the other with group control. This situation would permit the sacred to constitute a critical valuation of the profane where they were in conflict, precisely the situation for the major religious traditions in contemporary society that we have been examining. Closeness to this quadrant would permit us at least the beginnings of such criticism. Thus the grid/group analysis has perhaps been advanced to the point where we can begin to utilize it for our evaluative purposes, drawing on this suggestive set of possibilities.

Mary Douglas has located the religions of various primitive societies around the squares *A, B,* and *D,* especially squares *A* and *D.* This work is based on various anthropological observations, and it indicates that individuals in these small traditional societies negotiate group pressure, or negotiate directly for position within society. If we attempt to locate the major religious traditions in this scheme, great complications are immediately evident, caused partly by the longevity of these traditions and the fact that these religions are practiced in remarkably diverse societies. There are also complications arising from the fact that pure theology may be compromised by historical pressures. Neither Christianity nor Marxism, for example, has produced in secular practice large conclaves of equals, although such conclaves may seem essential to their original doctrine. Therefore it is not clear where Christianity or Marxism should be placed on the graph of grid and group pressures; whether they should be placed in terms of current civil expression, or in terms of idealized group loyalties. The correlation of placement with our remarks about the significance of location on the graph, as well as with the suggestive and predictive consequences of graph placement that have been sketched by Mary Douglas, make this a delicate matter.[30] There is also the historical dimension. Let us consider early Christian groups and Christians in modern industrial societies. The early pressure would have been group pressure primarily, caused by Christian family and local backgrounds, placing a person in the lower right-hand quadrant. Oppositional status within the Roman Empire would have resulted in diverse pressures directed toward the ego line.

I propose now to cut through the complexities. Let us return to our original two groupings. Clearly Hinduism, associated primarily with India and the caste system historically, is a good example of high grid, low group pressure. As we have seen, everything is caught up within this system, and the system has no precise boundary, as indicated by the lack of distinction between sacred and profane texts. Buddhism, in loosening the caste system, moves downgrid. Insofar as Buddhism recognizes the vehicles, it also draws a clearer group boundary. Functioning as a religion of choice in a modern industrial civilization, Buddhism can approach the upper right-hand quadrant, in providing a critique of surrounding secular society. Historical Judaism, associated primarily with Israel, is a good example of high group, low grid pressure. Judaism itself may enter the upper right-hand quadrant when Jews feel themselves to be isolated within a surrounding secular society, but subject to that society's secular demands. Spreading from Judaism, but retaining very similar features of boundary and internal purity, are historical versions of Christianity, Islam, and Marxism. Adherents of any of these religions may also find themselves isolated within a surrounding civil society, and belonging to versions of their religion drawing more or less closed boundaries around adherents. Thus we find versions of all of the major monotheistic religions growing from the lower right-hand quadrant toward the ego line as their adherents exist within societies that place constraints on their behavior potentially at odds with their religious convictions. The historical *tendency* for Islam and Marxism to be associated with nationalisms, except for short periods of power seizure and preparation for that seizure, and for both to downplay the notion of individual sin and individual redemption, suggests that Christianity and Judaism may have the strongest feelers growing into square C that are easily identifiable in history.

Let us consider further the place of religious groups within larger secular structures. In Europe, many nations had official and majoritarian Christian religions whose members could fulfill both civil and religious duties along lines of compromise worked out by the two sets of authorities. But in many cases, the compromises meant interpenetration of the sacred and secular spheres, the sacred legitimating the secular, and the secular protecting the legitimacy of the sacred. The religious institution was separate, but it left a definite mark on civil authority.[31] In some cases, as in the case of the Church of England, the compromises and interpenetration were explicitly set out. Religious toleration meant the toleration of minority religions. A member of a minority religion might experience more inconvenience in fulfilling religious or civil duties, but that was viewed as the price of minority status. Where there is interpenetration and tolerance, the potential conflict of sacred and secular can be muted by the parceling out of time and activities, and the partial consistency of complex civil and religious codes. Under these circumstances, the church can still function as an institution embodying group religious pressure.

There is the possibility, however, that civil and religious duty can come into conflict. If civil duty itself could become religious, the potential clash of two religious codes might not be so easy to restrain. In such a case, the situation in the upper right-hand quadrant may be better imagined as two sheets forced slightly apart, each sheet containing a representation of strong religious pressure. This can be given a historical description in the following way. Suppose that the movement of a society in the past had been into an area of high grid and high group pressure, and that this complex pattern of pressures had been manageable by a religious tradition. This can be the case even if the tradition is contradictory, provided that the contradictions can be handled. Now let us suppose that the contradictions are relaxed by splitting the previous religion into two parts, one of which has high grid pressure and the other high group pressure. These new religions might be more internally consistent than the original religious tradition, and hence the two traditions might come into more open conflict, placing very highly contradictory total pressures on the individual, suggesting that some change was required to handle the new problems that had been at least partially concealed in the older tradition. The more consistent the pressures pushing in different directions on the two sheets became, the more clearly compromise might break down as a means of dealing with the situation, and the more clearly some social change would be called for. The conflict would be more open, and hence more difficult to resolve by interpretation, particularly if each theology pressed for inclusiveness. The sheets could be thought of as even more distinctly separated. Theoretically, we could have open conflict that would be nearly impossible to resolve short of sacred/secular schizophrenia. In the next chapter, we will look at this possibility in the United States, arguing that a civil religion established to handle religious diversity as part of the founding vision came into open conflict with the religious message of major denominational religions. The result was ultimately the defeat of the traditional denominations as conflict between two religions was resolved by keeping the demands of the new civil religion, and giving up the social pressures of the traditional denominations, marked by a corresponding set of social changes. Christian churches became accommodated by marking out a safe Sunday time in conformity with social pressure, and in doing so let go of their potential for critique of the surrounding society save for those willing to reconstruct the past. The sellout was more salient for many others, who passed over the conceptual resources of an institutional Christianity for the critical bite of more alien traditions. Liberalism, the ghost of Christian values, turned pale before the emerging lines of Marxist theoretical egalitarianism. For many, opposing religious pressures were resolved into a single form of religious pressure accompanied by a slide from square C into square A. We will now turn to the fascinating detail of this contemporary situation.

5

Civil Religion in the United States

CHAPTER ANALYSIS   This chapter suggests that the possibility opened up by the grid/group analysis in the last chapter can be discerned in the recent religious history of the United States. The first obstacle to seeing this is in identifying religion with the denominational churches, and opposing these institutions as bearers of religion to a secular state. What the separation of church and state has achieved is a shift in religious location that perhaps could not be established in European states where religion historically supported civil structure. The freedom of religious conviction was ultimately purchased at the cost of its relevance to daily life. Separation means that the demands of grid achievement could come into sharp conflict with older religious group loyalties. The inconsistency but potential adaptability through selection and construction of images inherent in the older European structures gave way to a pair of religious structures, each incorporating a somewhat more definite image than that projected by religion during the mutual interaction of church and state. But consistency means a loss of adaptability in this connection, as part of the apparent resources of the older tradition are lost to both sides in the division, and are much harder to reconstruct. For a time, at least, charitable Christian equality could achieve a productive interaction with a pragmatic capitalist inequality. The relative clarity of the newly privatized religion preempted the space into which socialism might have moved because of its established grounding in American history. Gradually, however, the relative weight shifted as civil adjudication of religious disputes and an emerging scientific consensus changed the balance of images toward dominance of the civil grid. The emergence of a civil religion has been noted by scholars, but it has been conceived on the model of existing institutional religions, projecting a God who protects the nation but imposes certain moral standards on its conduct.

It is suggested here that a civil religion is the major religion of the contemporary United States, but that it is a religion much more widespread and quite different in its content than previous studies of civil religion have indicated, and it can in fact be identified with a *developed* civil utilitarian individualism, a possibility that has been curiously neglected by investigators of the civil religion. Four features of this religion—civility, individuality, segmentation, and science—are sketched, and their inclusion in the civil religious structure is argued for by an extension of Mary Douglas's methodology concerning dirt and revulsion at conceptual borders. This suggests that this is the time to resuscitate religion as critique in order to provide an appropriate critique of ruling civil religious images before a unidimensional religion plays out the ultimately destructive consequences of any rigid system.

The treatment here concerns the legitimated values of the civil religion, and not the details of its practice. Mythical history and festivals are noted in the calendar of national holidays and their celebration, as past scholars of the civil religion have noted, but the religion permeates everyday life as primitive religions are said to have done, and religious observance is not to be held to institutional attendance or patriotic rallies. The use of the legal system and the acceptance of its results, as well as the acceptance of journalistic accounts of what is happening in the world, are part of daily practice, and there is no doubt that television watching is an important component for many people, in which they celebrate the display of important common values. Were the civil religion slightly more differentiated from daily life, civil servants could be seen as a priesthood, along with scientists and media stars in certain instances, but the situation stops short of this institutional comparison. These complications are such that it would be nearly impossible to isolate the relevant religious observances as sociologists have attempted to do for the denominational churches. The civil religion is primitive in just the sense that its practice is not sharply isolated from the other activities of citizens. Religious critique in this situation can only be achieved by detonating the dynamite available to religious traditions in their oppositional images.

SOCIOLOGY of religion has relied on the identification of church and religion. It can study the role of the church as an institution in society, and it may study the expressed beliefs of adherents of other churches; but in so doing it does not necessarily study the relationship of the individual to society as mediated by the religious component of culture. In the European societies where the sociology of religion began, the identification of church and religion was reasonable enough, since countries or areas recognized official church religions which served partially to legitimate the secular states that recognized them. But there is the possibility that the relationship of the individual to the state has undergone a pronounced shift in American culture, partially because of legal tolerance of diverse religious beliefs, and partially because of the sheer size of the American society. Were this true, the churches may have served historically to preserve the cultural roots of immigrants in a new society, but they may now have some other function in society. The religious component of American culture may not be coincident with church religion. That would allow one to retain the sociological intuition that some religion must reflect the values of any society in the teeth of a declining ability to articulate the significance of any particular institutional allegiance. Such a possibility is the core of these last considerations.

Denominational differences no doubt once reflected differences in societal structure, and the pattern of conflict with other societies.[1] In America, these distinctions are no longer relevant. The situations of the churches in a society that permits their differences reduces those differences to something inessential. Doctrinal leveling is an inevitable consequence. Church members will not be able to define their positions in relationship to the positions taken by other religions in many cases, because the doctrinal differences will seem meaningless when they are called to explicit attention. Church authorities will also find theoretical differences to have decreasing significance, a fact that puts pressure on ecumenical thinking, and supports moves toward larger bureaucracy and power through coalition within the framework of institutional secular society.

In a highly industrial and urban society with official religious tolerance, each person may feel free to choose a personalized religion, perhaps as a component of a personality whose features seem calculated toward professional and personal success. Religion is not forced to confront a hostile ideology so much as it must take on the trappings of institutional specialization to fit smoothly into surrounding society. The churches can promote religion as a human need, and church attendance and participation as the appropriate ways of fulfilling that need. This need, a need that is seemingly fulfilled by the satisfaction of particular requirements, may or may not be a real need, as opposed to a need generated by a deeper lying cultural outlook, such as the need for toothpaste and deodorants, a seemingly generated need whose fulfillment can also be made in socially acceptable forms through the choice of an appropriate commodity. Making religion congruent with church inevitably shifts the significance and focus of religion: what had been distributed as significant for all of life becomes segregated into a special compartment. Institutional specialization and the possibility of commodity religion are critical features of American society, and now of Americanized societies.[2]

Religions have not always been institutionalized. In primitive societies, there may not be churches, priests, or specially religious ceremonies. The sociological study of religious institutions may miss a modern form of noninstitutionalized religion, and in fact be studying a trivial relic. Transcendence of the biological by the cultural is a universal phenomenon, and there is no reason to suppose that the contemporary American experience is a counterexample to this simply because the churches do not provide a manifest symbolic transcendence. Religious institutions must enter into various relationships with other societal institutions, and they must develop economic, political, and administrative concerns, and in the process they inevitably become secularized. The sacred cosmos is handed over to experts, to theologians, but the entire operation is not pure, and ultimately the sacred reasons for secular decisions must become contaminated, at least in the eyes of critics, by secular avarice. We no longer have monks living in separation from society, but institutions whose tax status and educational extensions require delicate balancing on social scales. The laity participates less and less directly in the sacred cosmos, and the demands of its church become secularized when they conflict with the demands of surrounding society.[3] An antithesis between institutional religion and society can now develop, an antithesis that institutions may wish to minimize. The price of church and state separation is thus ultimately the secularization of the church in a society where institutional clothing must be measured in the market.

Institutional religions now exist in large complex societies with a high rate of social change. The routine problems of people drift away from official doctrine, as official doctrine is kept invariant by specialists. Churches do not take specific stands on social and civil issues except at the risk of controversy. People's concerns are met gradually by other institutions that are free from doctrinal contamination. Doctors, social agencies, the culture media begin to discuss acceptable standards of personal behavior in complete abstraction from the bite of denominational doctrine. Specifically religious beliefs become mere opinions which have no real relationship to the individual's effective priorities and everyday conduct. The official model of religion may be quite disparate from what is of objective concern to members of the religion. Any such analysis must still deal with the continued vitality of religious institutions. People attend them, in many cases in increasing numbers, even though this analysis might suggest that the churches should be withering away. There are, of course, several possible explanations, tempered by some recent statistical signs that the large churches are beginning to wither. But attendance, if it suggests that needs are being met, does not prove that primarily sacred, rather than secular needs, are the focus of satisfaction.

There are a number of purely secular reasons for church attendance. For example, the churches offer the possibility of a small community in which one may make one's presence felt, while at the same time, of course, discharging guilty feelings about one's treatment of, or treatment by, other human beings on other occasions. Sociological study of the expressed beliefs of those attending, or even expressed reasons for attending, may be trivial where such motivation plays a role, and the suspicion that religious observance is an irrational leftover in a scientific age may foster looking in the wrong place. The secular possibility is unconsciously dramatized by death-of-God theologians who may argue against other philosophical positions while looking for new roles for the church to play. This admission that God no longer speaks at the highest levels may be interpreted as a candid sign that the churches and their theologies no longer reflect the structure of a living society. Accommodation having been reached, the doctrines are useless unless they are developed for critical potential, directed toward a nonaccommodation that is ruled out for those speaking out of their desire for the acceptance of secular intellectuals.

There is a temptation to suppose that empirical studies could trace a connection between religious belief and ordinary action. Such informal reasoning is plentiful, much of it based on the legacy of Weber's idea that Protestantism is particularly closely related to the personality type needed for success in capitalism. In all cases, empirical research in America has tended to concentrate on possible relationships between the big three: Catholicism, Protestantism, and Judaism. Often this research does not coherently allow for such (possibly) related variables as social economic standing.[4] The asceticism of Protestantism (at least in certain of its forms) might lead one to expect hostility toward loss of control over the emotions, thus predicting low rates of alcoholism. But one might also argue that the greater pressures toward rigidity of behavior in ascetic Protestantism could force a need for alcoholic release, or a greater tendency toward severe alcoholism, where the pressures proved too great.[5] One might argue that Protestants were more likely to seek status as signs of favor and discipline, thus preferring job placements of increasing status over Catholics or Jews, ignoring the isolating effect of such placement from their fellow workers, as in a promotion to a foreman's position. But one could also argue that this is independent of religion, or that the great explicit altruism of Catholics might cause them to seek job advantages to help their friends and relatives. We have previously stressed the complicated linkage between theology and praxis, and it is no surprise that empirical evidence finds little real purchase on the relationship of religious belief to behavior, a position compatible with the secularization and homogenation of religious institutions, and an accompanying irrelevance of pure theology.[6] Herberg, in an important early sequence of studies, concluded that the denominations were being swamped by a common notion of the American way of life, an ideology overpowering the differences between the denominations in the calculations of ordinary life.[7] Further, the general observation that church attendance declines in percentage as one goes down through social classes suggests somewhat that religious attendance has a secular motivation based on display and exercise of status rather than on a motivation stressing sacred compensation for this-worldly suffering.

Some empirical evidence suggests that there is a shift away from a perceived identification with traditional denominations and their official theological positions toward personalized forms of religion, particularly among young, relatively well-educated persons.[8] For such people, true religious experience comes when one is free of the ideas and opinions that comprise formal religion. The formal assumptions of religion, the importance of belief in a supernatural being or force, may remain intact in spite of rejection of church attendance as a valid and important means of religious expression. Various forms of occultism and personal experience are important, which, if not mystical, are still not susceptible to articulation, and the idea that there must be more to religion than human construction remains constant. Such evidence is quite compatible with the suspicion that normal church attendance brings rewards that are primarily secular, so that a sharply differentiated sacred religious experience is privatized, and associated with experiences that cannot easily be articulated in the vernacular. We will have to turn away from empirical data gathered from institutional adherence to find the conceptual resources we need to locate the sacred, if it exists, that is not associated with church institutions.[9]

Let us return to the theoretical implications of grid/group analysis. Most of the small societies in human history produce pressures that are felt in squares A, B, and D, where group or grid predominate, or where both are weak. Perhaps square C is difficult to instantiate because of the potential *conflict* between strong grid and strong group which could exist here, for example, for those who see themselves as a persecuted religious minority within a larger culture. If this conflict could not be managed by those feeling both pressures by some form of specialization of roles or division of conscience, there would be a permanent temptation for an individual to lessen pressure by leaving square C for another square, in effect ignoring or moving away from one of the kinds of pressures felt in order to lessen the conflict. The universalizing claims of both forms of pressure may make their permanent tension difficult to maintain. It may also be that either group or grid pressure in C becomes weaker for some historical reason, causing a shift in societal pressure away from square C. There must be some reason why square C is not seemingly occupied by many societies, in spite of its theoretical possibility, and the difficulties of maintaining simultaneously conflicting grid and group demands may be among them. It may be that this tension is vital and propulsive, as when religious eruptions have an impact on decaying older societies.

Let us approach the possible tension in square C in terms of the potentially conflicting relationship of church and state. As a member of both church and state, or of a society in which both institutions produce strong coercive pressure on potential behavior, a person is subject to pressures involving both institutions which transcend the immediate situation. Church and state need not conflict. In situations where church and state are largely coincident, it is possible to have explicit accommodation and division so that the church lends sacred legitimacy to the state (provided that the state adheres to certain minimal standards of behavior) while the state protects a monopoly or near monopoly on sacred legitimacy for the church. This situation has existed, historically, in Europe, and elsewhere where nationalism has flourished along with national religions or religious variants of major religions, as in Islamic areas, Israel, and elsewhere.

The sheer size and complexity of the United States, its official doctrine of the separation of church and state, and the staggering number of recognized religions have changed the relationship of church and state that can be historically associated with the nation state. Instead of indicating opposition to the official religion (or one of the few accepted religions, as in nations where Catholicism and some form of Protestantism are legitimate alternatives) by not belonging to it, in the United States one may reasonably be expected to show normality by belonging to one of the myriad of divergent religions that are acceptable within the society. The sheer number of possibilities make blatant atheism or agnosticism a suspicious sign of deviancy. The United States as a political state is a vast expanse. It is difficult for the citizen to comprehend regional variants, whose differences in manner and speech are becoming swamped by media treatment. One engages the country, as a citizen, on a very abstract level, with very few intermediate groupings of any solidity. To be from a particular state does not connote attitude or identity, since high mobility and national issues have tended to rub out state boundaries except as encircling a current address. Religious affiliation in a stranger is perhaps the surest sign that they have fit into their social setting, and can be expected to behave in a quasi-predictable fashion given the civil religious pressures.

At the start, in the Colonies, local experience reproduced European experience, but the explicit religious toleration required for the union produced a new situation; the country and the church could no longer be coincident. One's country could make demands, and one could feel pressures as a secular individual, which were independent of the pressures produced by any particular regional church. Protestant interiority became the sole institutional posture available to all religions, insuring that their influence would not impinge on public cohesion. As a member of a church, one could have any private belief provided that it was independent of everyday economic life and could mesh with the private beliefs of other Americans. In business, by reflection, one could not coherently act so as to exclude adherents of divergent faiths, or at least not relevantly proper citizens of divergent faiths.[10] Immigrants could reproduce the situation of Europe in ethnic areas, but very quickly the generations moved into the American pattern in order to be assimilated, and to achieve success.[11] The separation of church and state, although it permits religious freedom in one's private life, and ultimately assists in the withering away of religion, passes easily through schizophrenia. Freedom of religion means that religion can't be differentially expressed in the business of pursuing a living without ultimately encountering the civil consequences of the separation of church and state. One should have a religion, but it can't have a public meaning, or clash with the civil calendar. The state protects the existence of the church in exchange for the civil emasculation of the institution.

In the broad sweep of American history, there is an early period in which church and state are congruent at a local level, and civic and religious virtues are interpenetrating, at least on the level of ideology. A later separation produced a conflictual pattern which ultimately resulted in the defeat of religious pressure and in the triumph of civil pressure. Religious pressure faded to expose the individual in the public sphere to the full pressure of a civil religion, a religion that simply crowds out vestigial institutional religion in public concerns. This is our conjectural termination of church and state separation combined with official religious toleration. But this process must be examined more slowly.

We have stressed the fact that theologies can be pulled one way and another to produce conflicting attitudes toward such issues as war and the status of women. Where religion is not institutionally separate from civil power, both may show this richness and adaptability. What is here characterized as richness seems perilously close to inconsistency when viewed from the standpoint of logic. *No satisfactory and successful ideology can be other than inconsistent, since only inconsistency permits intuitive adaptation to unanticipated and changing circumstances.* Even if the ideology is not inconsistent as a system, its resources will prove to be inconsistent, and must be handled carefully. Consider such a problem as that of welfare payments in our society. Welfare payments are required for the sheer survival of human beings in a society where charity is not the important business of churches and relatives, and where private charity could not reach certain individuals for lack of the relevant contacts. The optimal size of welfare payments should, let us agree, encourage welfare recipients to find independent income and leave welfare behind, yet allow welfare recipients to satisfy basic needs during this period of adjustment. Yet these requirements are conflicting, especially when mediated through bureaucracy. They should be low to encourage independence, and yet high so as not to debilitate recipients through malnutrition or disease. Debate can proceed from an attempt to conflate these impulses into a satisfactory strategy when intuition suggests that the current payments are not appropriate. A consistent ideology could go totally wrong, and lead to obviously wrong levels of payment without having the resources to correct calculation through intuition.

The inconsistency of ideology is not a matter of simple logical inconsistency, although it obviously contains the resources to produce logical inconsistency if constructions are not carefully produced from its resources. This notion of inconsistency must be distinguished from ambiguity or unclarity, which would result in unclear specific proposals for practice. Religion is not continuously reinterpreted as the clarification of an obscure text, but as the construction of more specific messages from a set of rich conceptual resources. In science, conflicting (but clear) theoretical patterns may provoke progress, and accommodate new data, as in the classic confrontation of the wave and particle theories of light. This is more analogous to the strategy of religious interpretation, save that the possibility of a new general theory within the same religion is ruled out by the notion of divine authorship for the existent images and their adequacy. A parable is not vague or ambiguous; it is a perfectly clear story. What it means for specific practice may adjust to a historical situation, or it may simply not be relevant to a particular situation. But if all the historical meanings are produced at once, or all the beliefs juxtaposed, inconsistency may result. Religion does not attempt to make what is vague into something that is clear, but to make what is clear into a suitable guideline for a specific practice. Failure to see this results from importing the logic of axiomatic system into an area where it is inappropriate.

In the separation of church and state, the ideologies associated with each may achieve greater consistency, since their interaction permits enormous adaptability. Early in American history, civil virtue had religious connotations, and religions provided civil patterns of behavior.[12] The good citizen cared for other citizens, and took them, as persons, into account in the source of paradigm business calculations. Church and state ideologies were only partially separate. All of this may have changed with notions of individualism based solely on private calculations of utility, notions that came to dominate the calculation of acceptable public behavior. During the nineteenth century, with the rise of corporate capitalism, public and private notions of virtue began to point in different directions. A notion of pragmatic individualism became central to publicly legitimate action while Christian charity (or a related notion) became central to privately legitimate action. That they can point in different directions is nearly obvious. Returning to welfare, for example, these attitudes can pull distinctly toward lower and higher payments, respectively. The tension between pragmatic individualism and Christian charity is potentially a very strong motivating source of thought and activity. Contradiction does not paralyze except in formal systems; it is rather a vital stimulus to new activity where there are real-life problems.

Church and state cannot remain totally isolated. Welfare payments, immigration, treatment of minorities, education, war, and so on, all raise issues to which religious attitudes have an obvious relationship. As long as church and state provide conflicting but partially disparate sets of values, the tension can be fruitful for providing social solutions. But the tension spoken of here depends largely on a balance of strength between an increasingly utilitarian civil vision and privatized religious caring. The strength of the religious system depended historically on European roots, or on inculcation within the family, but this collective strength inevitably declined with the secularization of the church and the rising exclusivity of scientific authority within the civil vision, except in the cases of those individuals who found private sources of religious strength. What seems to have happened is that the civil religion grew in strength, while traditional religions' pressure shrank into the opinions of private individuals. As the state becomes mediator of religious disputes, this process is accelerated, because the public domain of religious conflict can't be decisively won in terms of religious argumentation, which further diminishes the domain of religious influence. Public opinions of value need to refer to abstract standards of goodness rather than to roots in denominational dogma, and the result is that their force is diminished in comparison to pragmatic considerations, unless perhaps abstract appeals resonate sufficiently with vestigial religious feeling. The European conflict of church and state is replaced by an accommodation in which the bite of religious values on public questions becomes greatly weakened, and its invocation also becomes a matter involving apologetics.

In terms of grid/group analysis, we can look back at the history of church/state separation in the United States as follows. As we have already noted, square C shows a potential separation of grid and group pressure, somewhat as though it consisted of two sheets that gradually separate as one moves to the top right-hand corner of the square. Emerging grid/group separation is based on partly congruent civil and religious models for behavior, models worked out in a European context of nationalism. But as these models separated, each became more consistent, and the pair became less congruent. Civil religious pressure became largely grid pressure, based on expectations geared to one's economic and social position within society, and traditional religious pressure became group pressure, pressure geared toward a vision of caring, sharing, equal subjects before God. The tension between these views, productive of social progress fueled by individual initiative while it lasted, gradually snapped as religious group pressure retreated before the claims of science which had been enlisted in the service of the civil religion. We are left with a civil vision that is not entirely consistent, but is consistent enough to push primarily for scientific and utilitarian resolution of conflict as the primary ideological grounds for resolving public dispute. The churches are merely spectators in the actual debate, their members reduced to citizens whose public opinions may be informed by religious values, but whose opinions in operation are to be defended by their public consequences.[13] In the arms race, for example, one may calculate the probability of peace, or the probability of deaths, but one may not advocate simply giving up weapons on the model of Christian virtue without being excluded on the grounds of irrationality from the responsible discussion of what to do. The civil religion is triumphant, but it can't be found by a sociology of religion that examines church institutional membership, or by a philosophy that examines the logical structure of Christian theology.

The separation of church and state depends on a strict division of private from public space, and an agreement that one cannot impinge on another in a practical realm. This division is always endangered by issues that threaten the public with private religious opinion (welfare), or private religious opinion with public power (religion in the schools).[14] As a balancing act, it is difficult to sustain, although the division between private and public was clearly established in European history, and then seems to have been fatally weakened in the United States and an Americanized Europe. For example, most European languages coded the difference between private and public in the power pronouns, *du* reserved in German, for example, for the private sphere, while *Sie* was to be used in the public sphere. (God, of course, is addressed from the private sphere, where he is present, even though he is also publicly worshipped in church.) The shrinking of the weight of the private is marked by the obliteration of the consistent use of this distinction, and the fact that the private form may become the common form is less important than that the distinction is fading out. The family, once the clearly delimited sphere of the private, has been increasingly penetrated by civil power and civil "services." As in the case of the pronouns, the obliteration of the distinction may seemingly be marked by an apparently paradoxical linguistic expansion of the private, as in lowered censorship. [15] And, of course, the civil religion itself may be marked with some of the religious trappings of the formerly private sphere of religion, references to God or America's sacred mission, a direction of influence that masks the obliteration of the distinction and tension of an earlier situation.

The possibility of an American civil religion has been recognized for a long time. [16] Rousseau perceived the conflict between the demands of civic life and those of religion, and observed that Christianity weaned people from state goals. He advocated replacement of the universal claims of Christianity with a religion that would be sufficiently powerful to motivate love for one's country and its goals. Jefferson anticipated the current situation in recognizing that civil rights could be independent of religious opinion, and that diversity of opinion could be settled by common sense assisted where necessary by scientific opinion. The current discussions of American civil religion can be traced to an important article by Robert Bellah. [17] Bellah argued that there was, alongside the religion of the churches, a well-articulated and institutionalized civil religion that legitimated the American polity. His argument centered on references to God in our coinage and national ceremonies that could not be taken to be identical to the God of any of the official churches. This notion of God seems to motivate calling this appeal to higher powers for legitimacy a religion. Bellah sees this religion accepting a picture of contesting strength, but he does not spell out the features of the civil religion in any detail, in spite of his claim that it is well articulated. Further, if *God* as used in the civil religion can't, on analysis, refer to the God of any of the official churches, this does not mean that reference is being made to a separate civil divinity, but rather that an invitation is being issued to each private individual to replace this abstract place holder with a more well-known figure. Logically, this won't do, but the power of ideologies is not based on logical consistency.

Subsequent discussion on the existence and nature of the civil religion has not succeeded in filling in much detail.[18] We can see that other societies may have had more overt civil religions, as in the model of Shinto which makes the head of the civil state a divine personage. And in many nations in the past, the civil religion could be seen as the official religion, which in its civil dimension acts to legitimate the state. But the United States president is not divine, and we have religious pluralism. If there is a civil religion reflecting the integration of American society, it must be different from these models, and may possibly be unique. As the church religions aren't the cement of a pluralistic society, by failure of having sufficient scope, some have suggested that the legal order must replace it, fashioning the common properties of education and morals, and providing the ground rules for interaction. Hammond has suggested that the essence of the civil religion is that there is a God whose will becomes known through democratic procedures, who has given America a primary role in achieving his ends on earth. But this characterization is pretty thin compared to the exigencies of everyday life, and provides a basis for an appeal to unity only in events of such magnitude as war, or the ritual repetition of civil ceremony.

Bellah has discussed utilitarian individualism as opposed to the biblical tradition, as a system in which interest rather than conscience is the motivational spring. Neither system need be pure. Biblical promises can be interpreted to provide for earthly reward, and utilitarianism needs some form of moral restraint on the part of agents to make reasonable forecasts about the fuure. But utilitarian individualism seems not, by itself, to provide an account of social concerns or social goals beyond the resolution of self-interest, and it totally ignores the injustices produced by differential power. Perhaps because it provides no God, and fails to discuss social equality, individual utilitarianism can't be considered by Bellah to *be* the civil religion, but perhaps it is a vital component of that religion coupled with some obligatory gestures toward the equality of power and status that would make utilitarianism work.[19]

There is no reason to suppose that a civil religion should be any more directly tied to practice than traditional religion. If equality of power and status is an important aspect of the ideology, one need not suppose that in practice it must lead to the acceptance of equality except among those privileged to be considered in the practical reckoning. The doctrine of equality has always permitted unequal status for women and minorities without the religion feeling the strain, much as in the case of just-war doctrines.[20] We may expect the impact of the religion to be felt differently by intellectuals and blue-collar workers, differently when utilized by Kennedy or Nixon.[21] There may be conflict between acquisition and saving, as opposed to gratification, in the possible calculations of utility into an uncertain future.

How can any common features be located? One suggestion would be to look back to dirt as a clue to conceptual structure as it was developed by Mary Douglas with respect to the Abominations of Leviticus. If the civil religion has come to be the dominant religion of the society, with its impact on all aspects of civil or secular activity, we shall have to hunt it down in reverse, tracing hidden conceptual lines from partially inexplicable feelings of queasiness and disgust. By looking at the official expressions of the religion that are embedded in public ceremony, students of civil religion have captured self-expression too abstract to have immediate consequences in behavior. Can such a project be made to work?

A first feature of the civil religion that can be revealed by this sort of reverse reasoning is civility itself. Civility is made manifest by the discomfort we feel when one's religious beliefs themselves become the focus of public discussion. Dirty politics may trade on one's religious or ethnic identity. Public discussion requires laundering of this spectacle into purely intellectual (and inconclusive) debates about institutional positions. Civility is the obverse of missionary zeal, but it is not the same as open tolerance, which trades on recognition of the peculiarities of the tolerated. Civility provides a shield behind which private opinion can comfortably rest as meaningless. This aspect of civil religion has been given a careful documentary screening by John Murray Cuddihy.[22] It is important to see that civility is not merely the link between utilitarian individualism and Christian conscience, but is actually opposed to the latter, and is an expression of the former. The calculations of utility are not meaningful unless they are made by *independent* agents who are to be considered only in terms of the actual consequences of their intended actions. The moment civility is taken as a component of the civil religion, the situation becomes dangerous, as an innocent-seeming civility is linked to a utilitarianism whose consequences may seem to demand criticism in the situation of power inequalities in which it is actually practiced. The public virtue of the religion is to "fit in," and to acknowledge that others do. Civility does not mean equality, since it is compatible with great inequalities and their preservation. It is rather the idea that certain properties are private and should remain so.

Among the outstanding private properties are one's religious adherences. This is reflected in television, where vacuous religious programming is reserved for Sunday morning (or religious cable TV), but no abrasive religious opinions are introduced to explain normal actions during regular programming, unless attempts at crude humor are being highlighted. The link to revulsion is established by the embarrassment many people feel when religious motivations are introduced into political or academic debate. Dirty campaigns and arguments are precisely those that trade on the mention of such motivational sources and their consequences.

Civility is related to a peculiarly ahistorical notion of individuality. Cultural attainments and other individuating achievements are suppressed and their employment in general discussion resented. Even though success may be measured in terms of income, asking someone's precise income is likely to cause offense. Inherited wealth is concealed, and talk of wills and inheritance can be distasteful even inside a family. Differentiation by age and rites of passage are occluded, private, unless important for an official grouping, as with the Gray Panthers. Asking for precise age, except for publicly legitimate purposes, is aggressive, and even public agencies usually allow one to write down one's age quietly, as when filling out application forms. There is no special clothing, or appearance, for various age groups. Teenagers and parents tend to be viewed as having the same rights, even though the actual family power hierarchy may run in either direction. In many families, civility is stressed over particular codes of behavior. The obscurity of death and related topics may be due to the ominous reminder they provide that life has a very finite earthly frame. All members of the opposite sex are potentially available in the same pool of attractive possibilities, as in television advertisements challenging one to tell mother and daughter apart. Models on television can taste food and change their preferences for it faster and more permanently than human experience would suggest. They can just as easily find a solution to an annoying problem of odor, and by doing so become so attractive as to stimulate dating where loneliness had been. In a society ruled by civility, human nature doesn't change, even if the individual uses new commodities, and this atemporal civility is integrally related to the other aspects of the civil religion we will notice below.

Civility is not necessarily a loving or caring relationship; it is rather one of insulation. People don't have to care about one another to be civil. In theory, everyone is left the same, except for the consequences of agreed upon action. If Christianity really matters, civility is nonsense.[23] Individuals have a historical dimension. Before and after conversion or baptism, for example, they are completely different. Sin and its redemption play a role in one's current status. In the end, religion matters. We couldn't really stand seeing those we care about outside the circle of God's love and salvation. Civility, in driving religious concern into the private domain, must either defeat or conflict with genuine religious conviction. A critique of societies ruled by a civil religion of civility is latent in every major religious tradition we have considered.

As we have noted, civility and individuality are linked. The insulation of civility is reinforced by the insulation of individuality. In the legal system, individuals conflict, and their conflicts are resolved, even if some of the individuals (corporations, for example) are legal fictions. Diversity of moral and religious opinion may force the legal system to a larger adjudicative role than in previous societies, one that reflects the emphasis on individuality in its workings.

There is a relatively small amount of scapegoating in American society. Individuals are held responsible for their own actions and for the actions of those under them. The working of America and the United Way is traced to individual effort in advertising, as is the presence of pollution and forest fires. In this way, and consistent with the implications of civility, the civil religion is blind to the existence and possible variation of larger institutions, assuming that they exist the way that they do and that their success is simply a matter of the individuals who fill their slots doing a sufficiently good job. Large institutions are generally portrayed as *opposed* to individuals (except for these natural institutions) in drama, movies, and television. In films like *Star Wars* and *The Empire Strikes Back*, the audience is expected to identify with individuals who are battling large organizations staffed by creatures exhibiting the variability of insects or robots. But even these organizations are usually staffed at top by very human villains, underscoring the incomprehensibility of other sources of coherent movement. Such material can be read as anxiety before a technological future and a spreading bureaucracy and as a romantic longing for the past, but then most viewers haven't experienced such a past.[24] As part of the civil religion, individuality does not need to deal with such fears, any more than Christian theology deals with the actual presence of church institutions and their consequences. Revulsion in this area is more subtle than in the case of civility, since it is not machinelike humans or insect human societies that cause revulsion per se, but such societies (or their conception) that are not in the ultimate service of individuality. The robots of a deranged individual are not repulsive, they can be confronted and dispatched with pleasure. Nevertheless, we see one side as free, and are invited to link ourselves to the free individuals. Many constraints on our policies in the real world may have to do with this preference for a free ruler (and dominated subjects) over an ideologically totally dominated society (no matter what its individuals seem to be like).

Individuality does not entail sexual freedom, but a fascination with sex can be seen as a footnote to individuality. In the end, sex is something that individuals engage in, and it is a bulwark of last resort against the intrusions of mindless technology.[25] The aversion some have to the idea of test-tube babies may be traced to this concern. To be sexually attractive (as an individual) one may utilize a personally chosen selection of aids and attractants.

To all of this, religion has the capacity to return a negative. Christianity claims we are responsible for each other, and that individuality may not be pursued at the expense of others. Individuality and civility are compatible with inequality, but Christianity is driven theologically toward equality. The civil religion takes over a concept of individuality that is largely blind to group needs not legitimated by scientific calculation.

Utilitarianism is involved here in that its calculations depend on mathematical functions ranging over the expressed utilities of individual actors, utilities that are not to be made incompatible by inflexibly acting on rules of moral conduct. The various forms of utilitarianism all share this common feature. Individuality here means that we are primarily responsible for our own conduct, and must accept responsibility where it goes wrong. Civility, by itself, could exist between families, but in this structure it exists between individuals, even within the same family. This notion of individuality marks the public boundaries of a private space, within which a range of publicly acceptable decisions can be made, and is not to be confused with the Protestant notion that it is the individual, rather than the church or the individual through the mediation of the church, that encounters God directly. An individual may be egotistical, spending income only on number one, or altruistic, sharing with others. Neither is conceptually attached to this notion of individuality. The religion gives abstract rights of freedom, liberty, and the pursuit of happiness; it does not impose a living wage or duties to others beyond staying clear of their own private space.

Revulsion at the borders may be noticed in the incredible attention given to the grooming of the individual body and its right to personal space. The dirt of others on our bodies calls for immediate purification. No other society has probably ever pushed the cleanliness of each body as long and hard as our own. We sit carefully apart in restaurants and waiting rooms to preserve this isolation, and enhance it by the use of private bathrooms and private transportation. An accepted advertising aim is to kill all germs or organisms threatening the private body. Such needs may have arisen with the civilizing process, but they are carried to caricature level in many daily lives where advertising and financing can permit it.

Civility and individuality are clearly compatible, but the civil religious picture is not entirely that of a society of civil individuals. Individuality is expressed in segmented hierarchies that produce many local but insulated power structures.[26] These structures are what is noticed in civil life; visibility depends on being included in such structures, inclusion allowing one's individuality to have a coherent place to develop. Rather than dividing into a few social classes, America seems to divide into hundreds of small clubs. Americans stop short of encompassing the nation, except in patriotic rhetoric. Such a vision would overwhelm the sense of individuality. Rather, they see allegiances to work groups, family, and friends at the microlevel, and maybe to unions, churches, political causes at the macrolevel. Conspiracy thinking has developed to reflect this trend. The devil was once a person, now he can be a polluter or a communist, i.e., a member of an opposed group. Segmentation means insulation. Leaders of groups may not compete directly, they may likely go higher to make an appeal for resources. Groups are kept apart because resources are distributed through brokers, who settle apportionment in such a manner that direct debate between suppliants is avoided.[27] Abundance has permitted this system to function because of open anticipation, where politicians could represent themselves as seeking ways to meet everyone's needs. Fixed resources and demands for guarantees of resources could cause this to convert to a caste system, a factor of some importance for grid/group analysis.[28] Rules, rather than trust, enable such a system to work, making the game a relevant metaphor for the system's operation. Corruption, rather than stupidity, is perhaps the greatest threat to such a system, since it subverts the rules themselves. This may help to explain what some have seen as an excessive American worry about corruption, which can be accepted in some European countries as an integral part of politics.

The presence of segmented hierarchies ties into civility and individuality as preserving and legitimating existing structure. If Marxist class analysis is correct, for example, these hierarchies divide up class structure into intersecting small groupings that don't break neatly at class boundaries. This makes it difficult to discern such boundaries. There is no legitimate social conflict that requires force between classes, rather change comes from new allocations between segmented hierarchies, or the addition of such to the system. Racism and sexism can be seen as failures to notice groupings that do not fit into this system. Women and blacks and other minority groups are not segmented hierarchies, and they can't achieve a place by insisting on internal cohesion. Men, or white men, are not a hierarchy either, they have simply come to dominate, in most cases, those smaller hierarchies that *do* exist. Therefore they may perceive themselves as dealing fairly with minority representatives within their groupings, and not understand that the sedimented history of these hierarchies provides a general barrier to full social integration. The structure of a union is a good example of this segmentation, since representation will be most visible up from the rank and file into the management level of local companies, making it hard to see and commiserate with similar workers (even in the same industry) that are not attached to the local scene. No division just above the proletariat, so to speak, is visible, since the lowest salaried management levels are not necessarily in direct conflict with workers' interests.[29]

Everywhere within segments, ranking and hierarchy is natural. Every club has a ranking and a best player. Foremen, chairmen, heads spring up naturally as the first evidence of organization. Plays and entertainment are dominated by stars of greater and lesser magnitude. The constant temptation to rank within segments is the sign of the pervasiveness of local hierarchies, as is the drive in sports to alter rules so as to produce clear winners and losers. Ranking supports individuality in that it is individuals (or surrogate clubs) that are ordered, and frequently top ranking is associated with the appearance of fully developed individuality, a fact that is pretty evident in interviews with top athletes.

These local systems have no natural coincidence with national boundaries. It is necessary to emphasize that we are all Americans in wartime or under a perceived natural threat, an indication that the boundary is not a normal perception. People elsewhere are like us, and basically good. Situations in which they are bad or threatening can be perceived as a failure of leadership or as the consequence of malignant leadership. There is no general term for non-Americans; not even *foreigner*, since some Americans are clearly foreigners, i.e., not yet assimilated even if in the possession of citizenship. Advertising strictures against cheap foreign goods tend to suggest that what is *cheap* is produced by robotlike, underpaid workers, and hence cannot be trusted for very long.

What is not clearly connected with some hierarchy and leadership is repulsive, as are mobs attacking our embassies abroad or those destroying our cities from within. Individuality and segmented hierarchy blend to suggest a natural structure of committees and task forces designed to worry some problem around to an allocative solution. A country too uniform, or one with too much hierarchy, or one with too little, seems foreign and incomprehensible, or perhaps not really a country. Monarchy or any other single civil structure seems excessively authoritarian in a land of checks and balances. Thus a structural solution to the incredible size of America is read into other political structures as a mark of viability. Christian theology can be opposed to segmentation and hierarchy, taking us all as sinners but creatures of God, providing a source of critique for this massive civil system but in contrast to the institutional structure of most Christian churches which mirrors the institutional structures of the surrounding society.

In addition to civility, individuality, and segmented hierarchy, the civil religion is also premised on the existence of public knowledge, and in particular on the epistemological authority of science. Learning takes place in public, primarily in the educational system, and it is accessible to anyone who works at obtaining it.[30] Here the empty privacy of civility defeats any attempt at limiting educational opportunity to those thought gifted enough to learn anything. The point is that the role of knowledge biases the system toward inclusiveness and the provision alternatives within the horizon of its recognition of members. One can change roles quickly through education. This does not mean *low* grid, so much as mobility within a grid less hampered by caste, and abetted by civility and individuality. No country seems to support such a pervasive notion of do-it-yourself skills, as if a small amount of information or a step-by-step procedure could convert anyone into the equivalent of a craftsperson. Intellectuals are respected for how "bright" they are, and for how much they know, not for the depth of their reflection. Ideas are transferred as in a commodity market where the purchasers have instant profit for their investment.

Public knowledge depends on the idea that the schools and media can avoid bias and present the truth. If philosophy of science no longer ascribes a black and white objectivity to scientific truth, objectivity lives on in the civil religion. Statistics are used everywhere to define the properties of public space, as though this had but a single outline. A story is offered on television, and details that are added make it more colorful, but do not change its basic presentation as an item of objective truth.

The postulated existence of public knowledge makes unsolved mysteries unpalatable. Knowledge should be brought to bear on mystery. Quick and reliable solutions can be obtained through sufficient effort and the use of guided technology. What is not immediately intelligible and explicable seems suspicious or bad. The intrusion of the helping sciences into private life can only be justified on the basis that their work can be legitimated as authoritative, and that the consequences are obviously beneficial.

While Marxism may accept the consequences of scientific development, arguing only for a different means of distribution, Christianity must remain at odds with the exhaustive nature of public knowledge. The miracles, by definition, can receive no scientific explanation, but even if they are accounted for by conceding to the ignorance of the past or are given a symbolic treatment, the direct encounter with God through prayer remains, like mystical experience in general, inaccessible to public observation and debate. Christianity must be severely limited to reach accommodation with the universalizing thrust of scientific knowledge, as it has been. Violations of public knowledge need not cause revulsion so much as mirth or incomprehension, but these tokens place the violations on or beyond the borders of the conceptual scheme.

My thesis is that the sharp separation of church and state at the basis of American polity, and the subsequent development of this pervasive civil religion, have permitted both the civil and the traditional religious sphere to develop rather unprecedentedly self-consistent ideological schemes that are in direct potential conflict. Nothing is being said here about the relation of these ideological schemes to social reality, but they obviously are at variance with reality, as were the policies and self-descriptions of older religious nation states. Colonial political structure involved a notion of religious freedom and a religious notion of citizenship that was complex enough to contain the seeds of both religious traditions. My claim is that the conflict between the civil religion and privatized traditional religion became a conflict between civil religious grid and privatized religious group. As long as these were in equipoise, which for many lasted at least until the end of the Second World War, the potential friction was creative and energizing. There is no need for grid pressure and group pressure to continue to exist, and their equipoise may not be necessary for a stable society. Society can slide out of quadrant D, suggesting that its members are feeling the primary impact of a new structure of religious pressures. I would like to suggest that the diminishing scope of traditional religiosity has produced a slide toward grid civil religious pressure, a slide very disturbing to those who still resonate to traditional religious objections to the features of the civil religion. Allusions to the civil religion are constantly made in justifying current governmental action, a fact of considerable importance for individuals sensitive to the content of older group religious loyalties. Threats to religious values can produce a revitalization of religion, but not necessarily.[31] The question is whether the movement suggested here is (in general) descriptive or not, and whether traditional religions have been permanently savaged by this movement.

Earlier I described the contradictory nature of the conflict between civil religions and private religions as rich enough to provide justification for various possible intuitions about such matters as welfare payments, and that conflict in general could be regarded as potential fuel for progress. It would be possible to argue against the division of civil religious grid and traditional religious group that has been suggested here by noting that some Christians are opposed to "mollycoddling" in welfare, and that some non-Christians are *for* charity, but do not found that opinion in religion.[32] Here it is necessary to separate possible justification from confused self-perception. In the latter case, larger amounts of payment could be argued for, let us say, to stifle social unrest, but the constant pressure for charity exists in the Christian tradition, and is highly variable in the utilitarian tradition. Utilitarian calculations can be steered by the shadow of Christian charity without overt commitment, in an extremely self-deluding fashion. Further, there are, of course, those who see America as a Christian country, and define aspects of what I have described as civil religion into their versions of Christianity. From the analytical framework adopted here, this results in a historically retrogressive position whose tougher aspects will be difficult to justify from biblical text.[33] Clearly, there was a time when Horatio Alger stories could be written, and Easter and Christmas could jointly serve to weld together Christianity and capitalism. But can that be done now? Seriously? Church complaints against commercialism alone indicate that the religious perception is that parity (in general) no longer exists.

My account suggests that one trace of Christianity can travel into quadrant *D*, where Christians in the United States experience intense potential conflict between civil religious grid and private religious group.[34] But the separation of grid and group allowed versions of both religious pressures to develop that were more internally consistent than the single religious pressures associated with traditional societies. As burgeoning scientific legitimacy became manifest, private religious group pressure gave way for many, suggesting a slide to civil religious grid as the dominant form of pressure on individual action. The slide is entailed by the fact that private religious group pressure had "held" the consequences of the civil religion in check, but erosion of the power of private religion allowed the civil grid to become dominant. The result is a situation where the major civil religious grid pressure is too consistent in its consequences to deal flexibly with unanticipated situations, and too consistent to hide the harsh social consequences of utilitarian planning.[35]

I have suggested here that the largest modern industrial countries, but especially the United States, exhibit a new religious pattern. The civil religion exists, but instead of standing over and against traditional religion, it has replaced it as the source of publicly acknowledged values, the only source with a legitimating aura. One reason the older conception of civil religion was so hard to bring into focus is that this replacement status was not recognized, and the sheer extent of the structure was underestimated because the prominence of institutional religion was too obvious. But why argue that the features of civil religion that have been suggested here are religious features of society rather than aspects of secular society? One reason is that violations of civility, individuality, segmented hierarchy, and public knowledge are met with feelings of anxiety, revulsion, or incomprehension that can be methodologically associated with the aura associated with the borders of religious concepts. Another reason is that the history of these concepts has religious roots in which the resources of transcendental criticism can still be located, and the concepts therefore contain vestiges of views of what a better society should be like. Bureaucratic Marxism can be called to task by the original version of a classless society, and bureaucratic democracy by a Christian vision of mutual charity and good will. But the resources are diminishing, and they are becoming difficult to recapture. I have suggested here the legitimacy of a philosophy of religion that will recapture these resources and set them against the consequences of a phenomenology of current societal values. This confrontation is more important than the question of whether religion as critique is said to be in confrontation with civil religion or secular society. Without the confrontation, the ossification of social system suspected and feared by many writers and philosophers could accelerate. The confrontation and critique is still most easily achieved in fact by mobilizing the resources of social critique that already exist in the religious traditions, rather than by constructing fresh arguments toward social equality or inequality.

That the analysis of the situation presented here has some purchase on fact seems supported by the period of religious upheaval that nearly all authors have noted in the United States since the 1960s. The growth and relationship of the major denominations has shifted in its pattern, and many new religions have become visible. From the point of view urged here, this would be a natural reaction, even where it is not entirely conscious, to a perception that legitimated values were becoming too rigid, too unidimensional. Much of this behavior can be read as an attempt to find new religions to replace traditional Christianity, and achieve a new equipoise with the civil religion by means of a communal feeling based on new sources. This strategy has been much tried by college students, utilizing either variants of Eastern systems, or individualized and private religious feelings. On the other hand, conservatives and liberals already possessing political power have made appeals to restoration of older oppositional values in an effort to locate legitimate criticism. The strength of civil grid and its carriers, as well as the sheer size of the society, and the power wielded in the grid hierarchy, make prospects for calling on older situations obscure, and the strength of the civil religion depends partly on its incorporation of the privileged aspects of these older situations. Equipoise and change cannot be systematically planned for. What is needed is a source of social critique that one can commit oneself to without a sense of mere tactics or strategy. A philosophy of religion that finds validities and invalidities in religious arguments is consciously or unconsciously oriented in the same direction as the vector of local history. A philosophy of religion that will develop religious images and conceptual resources can serve an honorable and ancient tradition of religious social critique.

Notes

INTRODUCTION

[1] See [L8], the title of which is a succinct expression of the thesis that religion has become invisible in the denominational churches.

[2] This generalization is true on reflection theory, as well as in Girard's account of religion, perhaps the only coherent general naturalistic account of the origins of religion. See [G4]. The pervasive data supporting the generalization suggest that we retain it unless forced to concede on the evidence that there are societies without religion. What it means here is that we should look harder when religion seems not to make itself evident in any clear religious institution.

[3] See the various books and articles cited in the Bibliography, and the brief expositions to be found in later chapters.

CHAPTER ONE

[1] The situation is well represented in the standard anthologies used as textbooks in philosophy of religion courses. See, for example, [C1] or [M6]. In the familiar papers and discussions anthologized here, Anthony Flew represents an attacker of religious claims, arguing that they are not subject to verification or falsification, and hence are not scientific. Kai Nielsen argues that the meaning of religious statements must be given in an ordinary epistemological sense, and that religious statements can't satisfy this modest condition. John Hick argues that there is a form of eschatological verification *in the future* not disparate from the sense of scientific verification. Richard M. Hare's subtle defense of religious statements argues that they can be defended from the data by adjusting the generalizations that intervene between them

and the data. His version of conventionalism is a dangerous defense in terms of the power claimed elsewhere for the religious outlook. In any case, the circle of ideas represented by such positions is polemically static, and the content of the defended religious assertions is cautious and defensive.

2   [F3] is a study of the consequences of the apparent falsification of religious belief from the viewpoint of cognitive dissonance theory. It is clear from this that a Popperian falsifiability criterion for scientific statements will also condemn the retention of any belief with falsifying evidence as irrational.

3   [L9] presents a fictionalized account of an incident like that studied in [F3]. This account can be taken to express the viewpoint of the members of the sect. In Lurie's novel, sect members don't take their own religion seriously until circumstances force them to recognize that they are being studied by professors as a sign of the validity of their religion. When the spaceship fails to land, sect members become convinced that they were wrong to have expected a visible spaceship, and conclude that the spaceship did land, although it was invisible to them. They thus learn something about their religion. The logic of the situation doesn't seem to favor the professors or the sect members.

4   [P3]. In this paper, Phillips discusses the connections between religious belief and everyday life, as when the death of a loved one tests one's religious faith. This helps to attack the isolation of religion without falling into a pattern of evidence and proof.

5   [K2] represents a thorough modern study of the validity of the proofs for the existence of God.

6   Galton's "Statistical Inquiries into the Efficacy of Prayer" was published in the *Fortnightly Review* of August 1, 1872. It is reprinted in many places, for example *The Humanist* 34 (1974): 31–33. See also [B16].

7   [H4] argues that in a system of nine planets and thirty-two moons, only the Earth with its single moon has an exact total solar eclipse. This is too extraordinary to be due to chance, especially as humans are available to observe such eclipses. Surely God has planned it this way.

8   See [S20]. The shroud appears to be ancient and possibly to be the wrap of Christ after the Crucifixion, allowing details of that event and Christ's appearance to be recovered through physical evidence.

9   See the argument with Popper in [L1], where it is argued that philosophers should study normatively what ideally rational scientists would do, not what actual scientists as a matter of fact do. In recruiting discussions in my own department of philosophy, I have heard the opinion expressed (and supported) that Kuhn is not a philosopher, but a sociologist. This was part of a negative evaluation made of

someone who had used Kuhn's book as a text in a philosophy of science course.

¹⁰ See [M1] for a summary of this attitude.

¹¹ See [P5]. For a discussion and an argument that some of the Leibnizian features can be avoided, see [A1].

¹² See [O1] and [O2]. The basic thrust of these attempts is to argue that left hemisphere and right hemisphere processing of information is different, at least in the normal speaker of English. When the usually dominant and linear linguistic left hemisphere processing is shut down by drugs or meditation, a distinct personality and wisdom may appear in the right hemisphere. Differences in operation of the hemispheres can be established by normal scientific procedures.

¹³ Some scientists have speculated that the lateralization of brain function and linguistic processing may be different in different cultures. It seems certain that it is also different in left-handed and right-handed persons.

¹⁴ For a critique of reified social relationships in Kierkegaard, see [A2].

¹⁵ [K3].

¹⁶ See the discussion in [K3], pp. 82–97.

¹⁷ [M7] discusses the contradictory aspects of social life; for example, how exaggerated familiarity can be used to establish distance, or how the desired power of a ruler to settle social issues can be hedged in with isolating ritual. Murphy notes that values can be incongruent with actions, but are not irrelevant to them. See [M7], p. 218. It is clear that the use of religious opinions would be particularly vulnerable to mediation in the unconscious, resulting in apparently contradictory applications. [R1] has studied sanctity and ritual with a special sophistication in the functionalist mode. In its view, sanctity can be used as a counterforce to the centrifugal effects of lying, permitting a temporal space to be marked out within which social changes can be accomplished. The low material content of sacred text thus has a rational explanation as providing the canvas, so to speak, for moderate alterations in social structure. See [R1], esp. pp. 173–246.

¹⁸ See the important discussion in [C4]. Converse discusses the packaging of beliefs into clusters that can be accepted or rejected by quite different social groups over time, but which are necessary for the recall and utilization of abstract beliefs. He also studies the shift from abstract and articulated belief systems to concrete, clustered beliefs as one moves from small elite intellectual segments of society to larger social groupings. Politics, for example, is gradually identified primarily with local issues and a vague conception of the larger party identity in lower socioeconomic strata. This could perhaps be repeated for religious belief.

¹⁹ See Mary Douglas's discussion of the Bog Irish in [D7], pp. 59–76. Friday absti-

nence can be an important aspect of local pride in religious distinction that is not as important to the theological stratum, as the latter may be prepared to trade concessions in religious identity for social and intellectual acceptance. The upper strata of a social or religious group may be more concerned with appearances to other upper strata in related groups than with issues of pressing concern to the lower strata of their own organization. See also [W4]. In reply to others favoring a "modernized" Catholic Church, Williams denies that separation is a result of original sin, and defends the sociological role of religion in preserving self-respect in the homogeneous mass of civil society. Although the doctrine of transubstantiation has remained intact, Williams suggests that the sacred body of Christ is not as mysteriously present as it once was in an object that is chewed by participants, leading to a feeling in certain Catholics that they are outside the changed church, an attitude just as relevant as changing one's beliefs.

20 See [A5], a paper that presents itself as the first systematic attempt to carry out such a study.

21 This is an oversimplified description of the rationality of witchcraft which can be supported by African ethnography. Its purpose here is to indicate the possible rationality of what may seem at first to be irrational social institutions. The discussion to follow is heavily indebted to the work of Mary Douglas. Certain anthropologists may perceive heathens bowing to wood and stone, but this is not the native perspective. For an important philosophical analysis of symbolism in other cultures, see [S11].

22 [N3] is a relevant classic.

23 See the sensitive treatment of this theme in [B8]. Wittgenstein, in the *Tractatus*, allowed that the world of the happy man and the unhappy man are different, although the difference can't be expressed in factual claims. This is similar to the point being suggested here.

24 See [G4] and [C2]. Girard, especially, treats the anxiety before violence as the root of society, and the origin of the sacred. In his view, society is born when violence can be controlled by distinguishing between legitimate and illegitimate violence, the use of legitimate violence allowing control of illegitimate violence, and preserving social stability. The sacrifice, the original form of legitimate violence, gives way to the legal system in history. In either case, socially sanctioned violence then provides just recompense for the injuries suffered at the hands of illegitimate violence, thus terminating a potentially uncontrollable cycle of violence in a quid pro quo. From this point of view, society is born to control uncontrollable violence between individuals, but the source of legitimacy is typically mystified, giving legitimacy an aura permitting its dominance. Religion encapsulates this aura, typically in a sacred history of the society, a series of festivals commemorating the founding event, and myths that express the mystification in an acceptable form. Without necessarily ac-

cepting Girard's theory, one can learn from Girard that social mechanisms that are too easily "seen through," that did not possess a legitimating aura of myth, would have a tenuous hold on the allegiance of society's members, tempting them to a continuous adjustment of the controlling mechanisms. This is ultimately why religion seems imposed, rather than chosen, and why conscious choice would undoubtedly possess some steering from anxiety.

25   [T2] is an interesting attempt to spell out the deviance of the splinter within Judaism that develops into Christianity. Social criticism is always implicit in the stance of this group of origin.

26   The functional picture of religion has been partially punctured by studies of theological tension and splitting *within* religious institutions. See [D1], pp. 42–44. [H5] argues that religion, in withdrawing sanctity from human institutions, allows a social change to take place when necessary. This, obviously, is only a partial account. The possibility that religion was used to legitimate social protest at the time of the Reformation is discussed in [S8].

27   The seeming necessity of religious values, which may be derived internally in a religious tradition as a consequence of God's greatness, has proved troubling to philosophers. In a situation of religious pluralism, choice of a religion may prove as simple and without serious hazard as the choice of a commodity. But critique implies deviance and the possibility of social sanction. People do not lightly risk social sanction. The seeming inevitability of religious values can ground critique of surrounding society and the risk of sanction. In the absence of an element of compulsion, the motivation for acting on religious belief where it entails a cost becomes obscure.

28   Our notion of belief, as contrasted with knowledge, is not the touchstone of religious identity in many traditions. This has been conclusively investigated by Wilfred Cantwell Smith in [S13] and [S14]. In some religious traditions, proper action is paramount, the individual being free to bring various interpretations to bear on the significance of action. This is alien to identification through belief. Belief versus unbelief is related to institutional specialization, as selective internalization seems to require such specialization. See [L7] and [P8]. See also the interesting discussions of defining religion in [S12], especially pp. 1–52.

29   [B13] has argued that the mythic tradition preferred variation in the telling of known stories, enjoying this variation, while standardization of an accepted text and its interpretation resulted after the impact of the scientific revolution. Science has encouraged the dubious assumption that there must be one correct version of whatever is true.

CHAPTER TWO

1   This is obvious even to empirical inspection and description. See [G3] on vari-

ants of Islam, and [s16] and [s17] on variants of Buddhism. The survey of religious systems in this chapter is based on information to be found in representative texts in comparative religion such as [B15], [E2], [K1], and [N4]. Footnotes to particular locations would be tedious in view of the acknowledged generality of this information.

2 These features of pastoral religion are nicely delineated in [s10].

3 Important contrasts between Hebrew and Greek views of the world are catalogued in [B14].

4 Those worshipping the Golden Calf may have been worshipping fecundity rather than the object itself. This partial abstraction may have been a preparation for God's full autonomy. In any event, the severe prohibition of image in Judaism and Islam is designed to focus attention on God's transcendence.

5 God may not have a sensual form, although God could clearly assume one, and communication between God and man is not thwarted by man's corporeality.

6 See [R3]. The Babylonian Exile and the Destruction of the Temple strained the credibility of the priestly sacrificial aspects of Judaism. After the exile, priests attempted atonement for unintentional violations of the Covenant, but this was considerably weakened during the Diaspora. Identity and atonement had to be dispersed into local congregations and their observance of the religious calendar.

7 This theme has been apparent in critical theory, particularly in Walter Benjamin and Jürgen Habermas.

8 See Exodus 21:20, 26.

9 Jesus is often thought possibly to have been an Essene, that is, a member of a group in oppositional stance to the Sadducees and Pharisees. For a penetrating and subtle discussion, see [T2]. It should not be assumed that later means better. Christians see Judaism as a preparation for Christianity, but Judaism sees Christianity as a degenerate, pantheistic form of religion, or at least this is one way of downgrading the successor religion. The discussion here is not meant to rule in any way with respect to these attitudes.

10 Miracles are not unique to Jesus. Apollonius of Tyana, for example, is one of the many other miracle workers reported to have lived at the same time. The staying power of Christianity can't be due just to its grounding in miracles. Their significance, at a minimum, must have been important.

11 There is a useful discussion of this in [s5]. The Christian God does not envy human beings, and such special doctrines as predestination have the exact consequence of making mutual envy between human beings pointless. If the God of Judaism is personal, and the God of Islam a terrible power demanding submission,

the God of Christianity becomes linked to humanity through a relationship circum-scribed by reason. Christian theology is an attempt to clarify this relationship by using reason. This side of theology is crucial to the development of Christianity, in spite of the fact that intercession can be accomplished through prayer, or the activity of the saints. For many Christians, direct encounter with God is possible. But these direct feelings of the other require interpretation in rational theological discourse in every mainstream Christian tradition. The existence of Christian mysticism is not of sufficient historical weight to require a major modification of these general comparisons.

12   This picture of omniscience may be a consequence of limitations on the notion of logical possibility. It is possible to argue in modern logic that even an omniscient God may not be able to predict or anticipate every detail of the future. See [A1].

13   [W3], p. 29.

14   Correctness of interpretation of nature on a single level is a mirror image that develops in the scientific investigation of nature.

15   See [S2].

16   [S1].

17   This doctrine, called Hagarism, is obviously not pleasing to Islamic theologians, as it minimizes Muhammad's revelation in seeing it as a variant of older ideas. For an account, see [C5].

18   There are, of course, important splits within Islamic thought based on the correct interpretation of the Quran and Muhammad's views about his successors. The power of Islamic thought and its important oppositional status to Christianity and Marxism can be grasped in [S9], no matter what the orthodoxy of the text.

19   The voluntaristic Marxism presented here overlooks arguments to the effect that the classless society can't be hastened into being through effort, but, as with the other traditions, a great deal of complexity must be ignored for the purposes of this survey.

20   The objections of Durkheim and Weber can be partially internalized within less deterministic versions of Marxism. It is possible to hold, as Althusser seems to, that various aspects of society may be controlling in the short run, provided that the economic relationships are ultimately determinant. This would allow religion, or philosophy, to be the immediate motor of historical change (in a given social forma-tion) for a fixed time period.

21   Will human beings have to work in the classless society? And could it be fun to work there? Some Marxists have projected the development of scientific technology to the point where goods could be produced in sufficient quantities by robots requir-

ing little or no human maintenance. Should they fall short, necessary work could be shared sufficiently to avoid onerous drudgery for any one individual. That is, at any rate, one theory.

22   One's karma is the weight of tradition and habit limiting one's freedom at any given moment. Even good habits are binding. Samsara, the wheel of rebirth, produces karmic status at birth. Dharma is the name of a sensitive attitude (short of moksa, or release) that allows one to escape rigidity in one's practice. For an introduction to these and other concepts, see [P7].

23   See [P7] for a discussion.

24   [B11] presents a perhaps definitive account of this phenomenon in English.

25   See [M3] for an interesting analysis of the functioning of caste.

CHAPTER THREE

1   [S21], for example, on the basis of a statistical patterning of fifty societies, attempts to locate relationships between religious structure (i.e., monotheism) and the structure of the primitive societies in which these religious structures originated. Since Durkheim's classic [D10], reflection between social structure and religious structure has seemed a possibility in primitive societies. In later societies, such factors as tradition could interfere with the reflection. The spirit of Durkheim's proposal, however, may well be correct even for later societies, provided that sufficient detail is studied to avoid the obvious pitfall that different societies seem reflected into religions of the same name.

2   [B10] provides an outline of attempts to reconcile Marx and Christ in the service of what seems to some a common vision of an egalitarian society.

3   [B15] provides a useful summary of the attitude of the major religions toward suffering and evil, a summary to which this discussion is highly indebted.

4   See [R3], pp. 70–72.

5   See [W1] for a discussion. Major texts seeming to suggest that universal salvation is a consequence of God's goodness (perhaps after an interval of torture or pain) are 1 Timothy 2:4, 4:10, and Romans 11:32.

6   See Luke 16, where heaven and hell are in communication, and Abraham contemplates the torments of the rich man as though they were completely justified.

7   See [W1] for a summary of Swinden's views.

8   [S4] is an example of an attempt to work out a synthesis that remains fairly

optimistic. For a more pessimistic version, see the discussion of Adorno's synthesis in this book, and references.

9   [L4], pp. 210–17.

10   For a discussion of this shift in responsibility, see [Y1].

11   See [S18] for a collection of papers bearing on this topic.

12   See the discussion in [B1].

13   [S18], pp. 4–5.

14   See the important article [T5].

15   [D9] discusses this point, arguing that the selection of environmental risk from other risks confronting society *at this time* requires an explanation other than an appeal to major religious traditions. Many reviewers have not been impressed. See, for example, [H1]. Some of majoritarian religious commitment have treated pollution as a purely scientific problem, one of rationally calculating how much money is required to attain fixed environmental levels.

16   See pp. 36–40 of [F2], and references.

17   This discussion is heavily indebted to [F2] and references contained therein.

18   See the characterization in Isaiah, chapts. 9 and 10.

19   See [E3], especially chap. 4, and [B9], for an interesting portion of the relevant history.

20   [C2] develops these ideas in detail. One should also consult [G4], where anxiety toward violence becomes the mainspring of establishing social order. [T6] argues for a general distinction between *structure* and *communitas*. Communitas does not merge identities, but liberates them from general norms. The complexity of modern culture refuses regular expression of communitas save in periods of war, except for cults that may emphasize communitas values. This would also be a source of religious opposition and critique of the sort urged for consideration in this book.

21   The following discussion is heavily indebted to [P2] and [R4] as general sources. Among associated problems would be those of racism and/or slavery. For an interesting discussion of slavery and early Christianity, see [S19].

22   [Y2] contains a useful discussion.

23   Wide reading about rural sects and cults in the United States suggests the possibility that the instrumental use of religious values in arguing for certain lines of action within the family may have been the only resource for socially isolated females after marriage, and their overt adherence to religious values, as measured by

some sociologists of religion, may be related to the strategic importance of religion in their lives. Primary evidence for such an opinion is not available in current research data because this possibility has not been linked to the sophisticated methodologies that would be required to find it in the data.

24 See, for example, the suggestive treatment in [R2], and the more scholarly approach of [B11].

25 The Decalogue, with its emphasis on coveting the wives of others, is clearly written from a male point of view. For the legal status, see [Y2].

26 See [P1] as well as other articles and references in the same issue of *Signs*.

27 [P1].

28 Discussion of the status of women in Islam, the significance of the veil, for instance, is extremely complicated. For some representative viewpoints, see [A3], [M5], and [T1].

29 Many societies have symbolized a difference between the status of the sexes by symbolic manipulation of the body, which, as clitoridectomy and circumcision show, may be directed at either sex. For an interesting discussion, see [H9].

30 Marxism has never provided a theory of the family, nor has it yet produced a feminist theory that can guide modernization for women. Until the problems of women and other marginal economic classes are adequately theorized, conservatism may seem more attractive to them than a predictable demeaning assimilation.

31 As a curiosity, some campuses of Christian colleges have banned dancing (but not kissing) during Lent.

32 In polytheism, gods may be more like humans, or less like them, so that dancing can be a common activity, or one that is used to express the temporal and illusory nature of earthly existence.

CHAPTER FOUR

1 Given what will be said below about the civil religion, these remarks are intended to apply only to contemporary forms of traditional religious systems.

2 See [D10].

3 See [D4], [D5], [D6], [D7], and [D8].

4 Chapter 3 of [D8] is the primary source. The abominations are to be found in Deuteronomy 14:3–20 and Leviticus 11:2–42.

5 This fact is supported by the well-known work of Claude Lévi-Strauss.

6 See the discussion in [S15].

7 Genesis 9:3. That plants only were the original proper food can be seen at Genesis 1:29.

8 See Genesis 1:29–30.

9 Leviticus 19:19 and Deuteronomy 22:10, 11.

10 Leviticus 18:6–24 and Deuteronomy 22:5 are relevant passages.

11 Exodus 23:19, 34:26, and Deuteronomy 14:21.

12 It requires some historical luck to be able to read back from abominations and filth to the relevant cultural boundaries.

13 This refinement is introduced with anthropological data in [D5].

14 See [H2] and [H3] regarding pig prohibition.

15 The origins of the blatantly peculiar expression "to sweat like a pig" are curious in that the pig cannot sweat.

16 See [D2].

17 See [D3], especially p. 501.

18 [L2] is a valuable discussion to which the following is heavily indebted.

19 [L2] makes the observation that frogs, not clearly land or aquatic creatures, have quite different culinary status in France and in England.

20 [T3] introduces its fascinating discussion with this riddle.

21 This observation is mine on discussing [T3] with various academic friends, although my friends may be united by various psychological disturbances that have permitted the friendships in the first place.

22 The example is from Mary Douglas.

23 See [H8], [N1], and [S7] for discussion and data.

24 The complexities are neatly disposed of in [S7].

25 See [D7] for an introduction, but also especially the essay "Cultural Bias," [D6], pp. 183–254, and various essays in [D4].

26 The notions of grid and group undergo shifts in Douglas's writings, and a quite casual inspection of the essays in [D4] will indicate that the authors have divergent concepts in mind. Perhaps the best form of these concepts for various purposes has

not yet been located. I have slightly adapted them here for my own purpose, that of making a comparative assessment of major religious traditions as well as an assessment of the current religious situation in the United States. This use of the concepts has not yet seemingly been tried, and Mary Douglas has used the concepts herself only to relate primitive religions to their surrounding societies.

27 *Restricted* is contrasted to *unrestricted*, and the terms come from Basil Bernstein. See the summary in [D7], pp. 40–58 and passim. An unrestricted code tends to be free from context, permitting one to communicate with strangers by elaborating what one means in a highly articulated style of language. A restricted code has, from the point of view of the unrestricted code user, a symbolic dimension, since its meaning will depend on context and familiarity with other speakers, or at least their social standing and importance.

28 This possibility is discussed in various ways in [D4].

29 See [G2], [P4], and [S3] for discussion. I believe the remarks to be made here are consistent with the discussion in these sources.

30 See the suggestive discussion of cultural correlations of graph placement on pp. 183–254 of [D4].

31 For a shift in values that entails a transition in Christianity from square C to square D in the twelfth and thirteenth centuries, based on a completely independent line of thought, see [N2].

CHAPTER FIVE

1 The classic source here is [N3].

2 [L8] is a brilliant discussion of the shift away from a meaningfully institutionalized religion in the United States.

3 Private prayer or meditation would cut against this claim, which simply notes the increasingly secular aspects of formal worship, and its insulation from other aspects of adult life.

4 There are many problems with determining effective membership or membership based on some rational assessment of theological differences.

5 See the somewhat inconclusive discussion in [T4], where differences between ascetic and nonascetic Protestantism are required to make plausible observations.

6 See [G5], [G6], [G7], [H7], and [L3] for a survey of sociological results. For a critique of method in such studies, see [P6].

7   See Herberg's contribution to [J2].

8   [G7] is a representative example of these findings. See also the more philosophical approach of [B6].

9   An extremely interesting possible analogy has been provided by John Kouwenhoven, who in a series of fascinating books has argued that art in the American setting in many cases emigrated from artistic academies, to the vernacular, that is, artistic modifications were made at the personal level under the less hierarchical control of American industry. Thus the United States may represent a social structure with a new secular and sacred pattern that eludes the confines of traditional European institutions. See [K4] and [K5].

10 Racism and sexism obviously cut deeper than religious differences, and in generalizing we ought not to forget that many specific local acts of religious intolerance occurred.

11 See [L3] for a discussion.

12 [A4] traces this development in interesting detail. See also the very suggestive [S6].

13 The inclusion of chaplains in public bodies and for offering prayers in public may legitimate debate by indicating that it is acceptable to the churches, not in conflict with their interests. But the chaplain speaks first, and when the debate begins the chaplain is typically not one of the debaters. Perhaps the most insistent assertion that religion is being replaced by national consciousness, with cults a sign of privatized religious memory, comes from Daniel Bell, who doesn't recognize a displacement to civil religion. See, for example, [B3], especially pp. 166–71. Bell sees the shift as recent. Others have argued that it occurred earlier. See [S6] for a discussion and references.

14 At the time of writing, the legitimacy of religious alternatives to the neo-Darwinian account of man's origins in public-school textbooks, public-school prayer, the intervention of the Moral Majority in political questions, the stand of Catholic bishops on the nuclear freeze, and the announcement that some churches were offering sanctuary to South American political refugees had recently been hotly debated, a sign that the necessity to keep religion in its (private) place was still strongly felt in many quarters. The presupposition of debate, of course, is that religion *has* been in its place.

15 For example, language and treatment of sex, once legitimately considered strictly private matters, have become more public in their expression in films, television, and magazines. It is not hopelessly dialectical to see this expansion of freedom in fact as the reverse; the invasion and displacement of the private.

[16] See the penetrating essay [L5], which traces the notion to Rousseau. By contrast, [W6] argues that Machiavelli's civil religion, based on the ceremonies of republican Rome (Christianity was too concentrated on the afterlife for the purpose), is a forerunner of American civil religion. Machiavelli had been concerned with curbing public corruption.

[17] The article is Bellah's "Civil Religion in America." See [B5]. See also discussion in [B7], [C3], [J2], and [M2].

[18] See [B7] and [J2]. [F4] attempts to test Bellah's assertions about the civil religion against "honor America day" ceremonial rhetoric on the Fourth of July. The expected assertions about America as God's instrument were scarce, a fact not surprising if the civil religion is interpreted as it is below.

[19] [B4] and [B5] recognize utilitarianism as an ideology opposed to Christianity, but refrain from linking it explicitly to the civil religion.

[20] Separate space can be justified by a "protected because weaker" status quite in conformity with theoretical equality.

[21] See the fascinating observations in [M4].

[22] [C6].

[23] The conflict between various aspects of the civil religion and religious conviction will be traced here only for the case of Christianity, as a simplifying measure, but as one reflecting the important historical confrontation.

[24] [J1] contains a discussion of *Star Wars* and *The Empire Strikes Back* based on future anxiety.

[25] Sex as constant on the level of individuality turns up in fascinating ways. For example, in the movie *Time After Time*, H. G. Wells arrives via time machine in modern San Francisco to notice the failure of his predicted socialist utopia to materialize, but not the failure of free love. He immediately falls in love in the time-honored manner. (Observation due to Joseph Sobran, CBS radio "Spectrum," 1980.)

[26] This idea of segmentation in American society is indebted to [L6] and [W4]. [W4] is especially comprehensive.

[27] The pervasive nature of this form of distribution, familiar to all academics certainly, is brilliantly sketched in [W4].

[28] Many predictions of fascism or collapse of ego in the United States may be based on extrapolation of structure in the opposite direction. Hinduism, which is here compared to American civil religion, is noteworthy in terms of the size of area and population of origin.

29 More recently, the work site as a neutral place for socialization has become an acceptable topic of public discussion. The shift to work sites from family settings on television series displays this situation nicely, as Jennifer McErlean has pointed out in conversation.

30 The enormous size of higher education in the United States couldn't be based on the Jeffersonian principle that democracy required informed voters, since much of the curriculum has no obvious practical consequence. What is said here is partially counterexampled by past (and present) exclusions of minorities, but they have had no obvious visible place in the system.

31 [F1] makes a proposal suggesting the inevitability of desecularization. Obviously, as noted below, some people will react in this fashion, but there is no necessity about the mechanism involved. It would also be possible to argue that the decline of traditional religion is good for it, making it clear that worldly accommodation shouldn't be its goal.

32 I am indebted to an anonymous referee of a paper I submitted to *Sociological Analysis* for this point.

33 For illustrative purposes, there is [B2]. Barton's extroverted, ebullient Christ has not proved congenial to orthodox Christianity, where the image of sorrow and agony preserves a moment of potential criticism.

34 South American Liberation Theology is sufficient to show that Christianity has other traces. Of course, private religious group pressure in the United States setting could also be experienced as Jewish or Islamic group pressure; other possibilities are also plentiful. "God is dead" theology seems a possible intuition of the slide I suggest in the context of the United States.

35 Russia also exists as a large industrialized society. It is important to wonder whether the vision of the classless society and the loving equality of humanity has been as overwhelmed as the Christian kernel inside Western society as an ameliorating factor in social calculation. What, besides considerations of cost, can be effectively weighed against arms expansion in either country?

Bibliography

[A1] Ackermann, Robert. "An Alternative Free Will Defense." *Religious Studies* 18 (1982): 362–372.

[A2] Adorno, Theodore W. "On Kierkegaard's Doctrine of Love." *Zeitschrift für Sozialforschung* 8 (1940): 413–429.

[A3] Ahmed, Leila. "Western Ethnocentrism and Perceptions of the Harem." *Feminist Studies* 8 (1982): 521–533.

[A4] Arieli, Yehoshua. *Individualism and Nationalism in American Ideology.* Cambridge: Harvard University Press, 1964.

[A5] Azzi, Corry, and Ehrenberg, Ronald. "Household Allocation of Time and Church Attendance." *Journal of Political Economy* 83 (1975): 27–56.

[B1] Barr, James. "Man and Nature: The Ecological Controversy and the Old Testament." Pp. 48–75 of [S18].

[B2] Barton, Bruce. *The Man Nobody Knows.* Indianapolis: Bobbs-Merrill Co., 1925.

[B3] Bell, Daniel. *The Cultural Contradictions of Capitalism.* New York: Basic Books, 1978.

[B4] Bellah, Robert N. *The Broken Covenant.* New York: Seabury Press, 1975.

[B5] Bellah, Robert N. "Civil Religion in America." *Daedalus* 96 (1967): 1–21. (Reprinted in [J2].)

[B6] Bellah, Robert N. "New Religious Consciousness." *New Republic* 171 (November 23, 1974): 33–41.

[B7] Bellah, Robert N., and Hammond, Phillip E. *Varieties of Civil Religion.* New York: Harper and Row, 1980.

[B8] Bennett, Charles A. *The Dilemma of Religious Knowledge*. New Haven: Yale University Press, 1931.

[B9] Bennigsen, Alexandre A., and Wimbush, S. Enders. *Muslim National Communism in the Soviet Union*. Chicago: University of Chicago Press, 1979.

[B10] Bentley, James. *Between Marx and Christ: The Dialogue in German-Speaking Europe, 1870–1970*. London: New Left Books, 1982.

[B11] Bharati, Agehananda. *The Ochre Robe*. New York: Doubleday and Co., 1970. (Original edition, 1962.)

[B12] Bharati, Agehananda. *The Tantric Tradition*. New York: Doubleday and Co., 1970.

[B13] Blumenberg, Hans. "Wirklichkeitsbegriff und Wirkungspotential des Mythos." Pp. 11–66 of Fuhrmann, Manfred, hrsg., *Terror und Spiel*, Munich: W. Fink Verlag, 1971.

[B14] Boman, Thorleif. *Hebrew Thought Compared with Greek*. New York: W. W. Norton, 1970. (Original German edition, 1954.)

[B15] Bowker, John. *Problems of Suffering in Religions of the World*. Cambridge: Cambridge University Press, 1970.

[B16] Brush, Stephen. "The Prayer Test." *American Scientist* 62 (1974): 561–563.

[C1] Cahn, Steven, ed. *Philosophy of Religion*. New York: Harper and Row, 1970.

[C2] Callois, Roger. *Man and the Sacred*. Glencoe, Illinois: Free Press, 1959. (Original French edition, 1950.)

[C3] Coleman, John A. "Civil Religion." *Sociological Analysis* 31 (1970): 67–77.

[C4] Converse, Philip E. "The Nature of Belief Systems in Mass Publics." Pp. 206–261 of Apter, David E., ed., *Ideology and Discontent*, Glencoe, Illinois: Free Press, 1964.

[C5] Crone, Patricia, and Cook, Michael. *Hagarism: The Making of the Muslim World*. Cambridge: Cambridge University Press, 1974.

[C6] Cuddihy, John Murray. *No Offense: Civil Religion and Protestant Taste*. New York: Seabury Press, 1978.

[D1] Desroche, Henri. *Jacob and the Angel*. Amherst: University of Massachusetts Press, 1973. (Original French edition, 1968.)

[D2] Diener, Paul; Moore, Kent; and Mutaw, Robert. "Meats, Markets, and Mechanical Materialism: The Great Protein Fiasco in Anthropology." *Dialectical Anthropology* 5 (1980): 171–192.

[D3] Diener, Paul, and Robkin, Eugene E. "Ecology, Evolution, and the Search for Cultural Origins: The Question of Islamic Pig Prohibition." *Current Anthropology* 19 (1978): 493–540.

[D4] Douglas, Mary, ed. *Essays in the Sociology of Perception*. London: Routledge and Kegan Paul, 1982.

[D5] Douglas, Mary. *Implicit Meanings*. London: Routledge and Kegan Paul, 1978.

[D6] Douglas, Mary. *In the Active Voice*. London: Routledge and Kegan Paul, 1982.

[D7] Douglas, Mary. *Natural Symbols*. London: Barrie and Jenkins, 1970.

[D8] Douglas, Mary. *Purity and Danger*. London: Routledge and Kegan Paul, 1978. (Original edition, 1966.)

[D9] Douglas, Mary, and Wildavsky, Aaron. *Risk and Culture*. Berkeley: University of California Press, 1982.

[D10] Durkheim, Emile. *The Elementary Forms of the Religious Life*. New York: Free Press, 1965. (Original French edition, 1912.)

[E1] Eister, Allan W., ed. *Changing Perspectives in the Scientific Study of Religion*. New York: John Wiley and Sons, 1964.

[E2] Ellwood, Robert S. *Many Peoples, Many Faiths*. Englewood Cliffs, New Jersey: Prentice-Hall, 1976.

[E3] Enayat, Hamid. *Modern Islamic Political Thought*. Austin: University of Texas Press, 1982.

[F1] Fenn, Richard K. *Toward a Theory of Secularization*. Chicago: Society for the Scientific Study of Religion Monograph Series, 1978.

[F2] Ferguson, John. *War and Peace in the World's Religions*. New York: Oxford University Press, 1978.

[F3] Festinger, Leon; Riecken, Henry W.; and Schacter, Stanley. *When Prophecy Fails*. New York: Harper and Row, 1956.

[F4] Flippen, Charles C., and Thomas, Michael C. "American Civil Religion: An Empirical Study." *Social Forces* 51 (1972): 218–225.

[G1] Galton, Sir Francis. "Statistical Inquiries into the Efficacy of Prayer." Reprinted in *The Humanist* 34 (1974): 31–33.

[G2] Gaylin, Willard. *Feelings: Our Vital Signs*. New York: Harper and Row, 1979.

[G3] Geertz, Clifford. *Islam Observed*. Chicago: University of Chicago Press, 1971.

[G4] Girard, René. *Violence and the Sacred*. Baltimore: The Johns Hopkins University Press, 1977. (Original French edition, 1972.)

[G5] Glock, Charles Y., ed. *Religion in Sociological Perspective*. Belmont, California: Wadsworth, 1973.

164

[G6] Glock, Charles, and Stark, Rodney. *Religion and Society in Tension*. Chicago: Rand McNally and Co., 1965.

[G7] Glock, Charles Y., and Wuthnow, Robert. "God in the Gut." *Psychology Today* 7 (1974): 131–136.

[H1] Hacking, Ian. "Why Are You Scared?" Review of [D9]. *New York Review of Books* 37 (September 23, 1982): 30–33.

[H2] Harris, Marvin. *Cannibals and Kings*. New York: Random House, 1977.

[H3] Harris, Marvin. *Cows, Pigs, Wars, and Witches: The Riddles of Culture*. New York: Random House, 1974.

[H4] Hart, Richard, and Mendillo, Michael. "Total Solar Eclipses, Extraterrestrial Life, and the Existence of God." Excerpted in *Physics Today* 27 (1974): 73.

[H5] Harvey, Van A. "Some Aspects of Peter Berger's Theory of Religion." *Journal of the American Academy of Religion* 41 (1973): 75–93.

[H6] Herberg, Will. "America's Civil Religion: What It Is and Whence It Comes." Pp. 76–88 of [J2].

[H7] Herberg, Will. *Protestant—Catholic—Jew*. New York: Doubleday and Co., 1960.

[H8] Hertz, Robert. *Right and Left*. Chicago: University of Chicago Press, 1973.

[H9] Hosken, Fran P. "Female Genital Mutilation and Human Rights." *Feminist Issues* 1 (1981): 3–23.

[J1] Jennings, Christopher. "Mirrors of Reality." *Science for the People* 12 (1980): 27–29.

[J2] Jones, Donald G., and Richey, Russell E., eds. *American Civil Religion*. New York: Harper and Row, 1974.

[K1] Kaufmann, Walter. *Religions in Four Dimensions*. New York: Reader's Digest Press, 1976.

[K2] Kenny, Anthony. *The Five Ways*. New York: Schocken Books, 1969.

[K3] Kolakowski, Leszek. *Religion*. New York: Oxford University Press, 1982.

[K4] Kouwenhoven, John. *Half a Truth Is Better Than None*. Chicago: University of Chicago Press, 1982.

[K5] Kouwenhoven, John. *Made in America*. Newton Centre, Massachusetts: Charles T. Branford Co., 1948.

[L1] Lakatos, Imre, and Musgrave, Alan. *Criticism and the Growth of Knowledge*. Cambridge: Cambridge University Press, 1970.

[L2] Leach, Edmund. "Anthropological Aspects of Language: Animal Categories and Verbal Abuse." Pp. 23–63 of Lenneberg, Eric H., ed., *New Directions in the Study of Language*, Cambridge: MIT Press, 1964. Reprinted on pp. 39–67 of

Maranda, Pierre, ed., *Mythology*, Harmondsworth: Penguin Books, 1972.

[L3] Lenski, Gerhard. *The Religious Factor*. New York: Doubleday and Co., 1963.

[L4] Levy, Bernard-Henri. *The Testament of God*. New York: Harper and Row, 1980. (Original French edition, 1978.)

[L5] Little, David. "The Origins of Perplexity: Civil Religion and Moral Belief in the Thought of Thomas Jefferson." Pp. 185–210 of [J2].

[L6] Lofland, Lyn. *A World of Strangers*. New York: Basic Books, 1973.

[L7] Luckmann, Thomas. "Belief, Unbelief, and Religion." Pp. 21–39 of Caporale, Rocco, and Grumelli, Antonio, eds., *The Culture of Unbelief*, Berkeley: University of California Press, 1971.

[L8] Luckmann, Thomas. *The Invisible Religion*. New York: Macmillan Co., 1967. (Original German edition, 1963.)

[L9] Lurie, Alison. *Imaginary Friends*. New York: Avon Books, 1967.

[M1] Mackie, John. "Evil and Omnipotence." *Mind* 64 (1955): 200–212. Reprinted in [C1] and [M6].

[M2] Markoff, John, and Regan, Daniel. "The Rise and Fall of Civil Religion: Comparative Perspectives." *Sociological Analysis* 42 (1981): 333–352.

[M3] Marriott, McKim. "Hindu Transactions: Diversity Without Dualism." Pp. 109–142 of Kapferer, Bruce, ed., *Transaction and Meaning*, Philadelphia: ISHI Press, 1976.

[M4] Marty, Martin E. "Two Kinds of Two Kinds of Civil Religion." Pp. 139–157 of [J2].

[M5] Minai, Naila. *Women in Islam*. New York: Seaview Books, 1981.

[M6] Mitchell, Basil, ed. *The Philosophy of Religion*. Oxford: Oxford University Press, 1971.

[M7] Murphy, Robert F. *The Dialectics of Social Life*. New York: Basic Books, 1971.

[N1] Needham, Rodney, ed. *Right and Left: Essays in Dual Symbolic Classification*. Chicago: University of Chicago Press, 1973.

[N2] Nelson, Benjamin. "*Eros, Logos, Nomos, Polis*: Their Changing Balances and the Vicissitudes of Communities and Civilizations." Pp. 85–111 of [E1].

[N3] Niebuhr, Helmut Richard. *The Social Sources of Denominationalism*. New York: Meridian Books, 1957.

[N4] Noss, John B. *Man's Religions*. New York: Macmillan Co., 1974. (Originally published in 1949.)

166

[o1] Ornstein, Robert Evans, ed. *The Nature of Human Consciousness.* San Francisco: W. H. Freeman, 1973.

[o2] Ornstein, Robert Evans. *The Psychology of Consciousness.* New York: Harcourt Brace Jovanovich, 1977.

[P1] Pagels, Elaine H. "What Became of God the Mother? Conflicting Images of God in Early Christianity." *Signs* 2 (1976): 293–303.

[P2] Parrinder, Geoffrey. *Sex in the World's Religions.* New York: Oxford University Press, 1980.

[P3] Phillips, D. Z. "Religious Beliefs and Language Games." *Ratio* 13 (1970): 26–46.

[P4] Piers, Gerhart, and Singer, Milton B. *Shame and Guilt.* New York: W. W. Norton and Co., 1971.

[P5] Plantinga, Alvin. *God, Freedom, and Evil.* Grand Rapids, Michigan: Eerdmans, 1977. (Original edition, 1974.)

[P6] Plock, Donald R. "Religion as an Independent Variable: A Critique of Some Major Research." Pp. 275–294 of [E1].

[P7] Potter, Karl H. *Presuppositions of India's Philosophies.* Englewood Cliffs, New Jersey: Prentice-Hall, 1963.

[P8] Pouillon, Jean. "Remarks on the Verb 'To Believe'." Pp. 1–23 of Izard, Michel, and Smith, Pierre, eds., *Between Belief and Transgression*, Chicago: University of Chicago Press, 1982.

[R1] Rappaport, Roy A. *Ecology, Meaning, and Religion.* Richmond, California: North Atlantic Books, 1979.

[R2] Rawson, Philip. *Tantra: The Indian Cult of Ecstasy.* New York: Avon Books, 1973.

[R3] Robinson, H. Wheeler. *Inspiration and Revelation in the Old Testament.* Oxford: Oxford University Press, 1946.

[R4] Ruether, Rosemary Radford, ed. *Religion and Sexism.* New York: Simon and Schuster, 1974.

[S1] Said, Edward W. *Covering Islam.* New York: Pantheon Books, 1981.

[S2] Said, Edward W. *Orientalism.* New York: Pantheon Books, 1978.

[S3] Schneider, Carl D. *Shame, Exposure, and Privacy.* Boston: Beacon Press, 1977.

[S4] Schneider, Michael. *Neurosis and Civilization.* New York: Seabury Press, 1975. (Original German edition, 1973.)

[S5] Schoeck, Helmut. *Envy.* London: Secker and Warburg, 1969. (Original German edition, 1966.)

[s6] Schroyer, Trent. "Cultural Surplus in America." *New German Critique*, no. 26 (1982): 81–117.

[s7] Schwartz, Barry. *Vertical Classification*. Chicago: University of Chicago Press, 1981.

[s8] Scribner, Bob. "Religion, Society, and Culture: Reorienting the Reformation." *History Workshop Journal*, no. 14 (1982): 2–22.

[s9] Shari'ati, Ali. *On the Sociology of Islam*. Berkeley: Mizan Press, 1979.

[s10] Shepard, Paul. *Man in the Landscape*. New York: Alfred Knopf, 1967.

[s11] Skorupski, John. *Symbol and Theory: A Philosophical Study of Theories of Religion in Social Anthropology*. Cambridge: Cambridge University Press, 1976.

[s12] Smith, Jonathan Z. *Imagining Religion*. Chicago: University of Chicago Press, 1982.

[s13] Smith, Wilfred Cantwell. *Faith and Belief*. Princeton: Princeton University Press, 1979.

[s14] Smith, Wilfred Cantwell. *The Meaning and End of Religion*. New York: Mentor Books, 1964.

[s15] Soler, Jean. "The Dietary Prohibitions of the Hebrews." *New York Review of Books* 31 (June 14, 1979): 24–30.

[s16] Spiro, Melford E. *Buddhism and Society*. New York: Harper and Row, 1972.

[s17] Spiro, Melford E. *Burmese Supernaturalism*. Englewood Cliffs, New Jersey: Prentice-Hall, 1967.

[s18] Spring, David, and Spring, Eileen, eds. *Ecology and Religion in History*. New York: Harper Torchbooks, 1974.

[s19] Ste. Croix, G. E. M. de. *The Class Struggle in the Ancient Greek World*. London: Duckworth, 1981.

[s20] Sullivan, Barbara M. "How In Fact Was Jesus Christ Laid In His Tomb?" *National Review* 25 (1973): 785–789.

[s21] Swanson, Guy E. *The Birth of the Gods*. Ann Arbor: University of Michigan Press, 1968.

[t1] Tabari, Azar. "The Enigma of the Veiled Iranian Woman." *Merip Reports* 12 (1982): 22–33.

[t2] Theissen, Gerd. *Sociology of Early Palestinian Christianity*. Philadelphia: Fortress Press, 1978. (Original German edition, 1977.)

[t3] Thompson, Michael. *Rubbish Theory*. Oxford: Oxford University Press, 1979.

[t4] Thorner, Isidor. "Ascetic Protestantism and Alcoholism." *Psychiatry* 16 (1953): 167–176.

168

[T5] Tuan, Yi-Fu. "Discrepancies between Environmental Attitude and Behavior: Examples from Europe and China." Pp. 91–113 of [S18].

[T6] Turner, Victor. "Metaphors of Anti-Structure in Religious Culture." Pp. 63–84 of [E1].

[W1] Walker, D. P. *The Decline of Hell*. Chicago: University of Chicago Press, 1964.

[W2] Wallace, Anthony F. C. *Religion: An Anthropological View*. New York: Random House, 1966.

[W3] Walzer, Michael. *The Revolution of the Saints*. New York: Atheneum, 1970.

[W4] Wiebe, Robert H. *The Segmented Society*. Oxford: Oxford University Press, 1979. (Original edition, 1975.)

[W5] Williams, Paul. "A Rebuke of a Rejoinder." *National Review* 29 (1977): 270–271.

[W6] Wolin, Sheldon S. "America's Civil Religion." *Democracy* 2 (1982): 7–17.

[Y1] Young, R. V., Jr. "Christianity and Ecology." *National Review* 26 (1974): 1454–1458, 1477, and 1479.

[Y2] Yuval-Davis, Nira. "The Bearers of the Collective: Women and Religious Legislation in Israel." *Feminist Review*, no. 4 (1980): 15–27.

Index

Abominations of Leviticus, 87–94, 131, 154–55
Adam and Eve, fall of, 65, 106
agency, as assumed in monotheism, 32–33, 49
ahimsa, 70
animal names and dietary assumptions, 93–94
atonement, 60–61

belief systems, as criteria for orthodoxy, 42, 47–48, 149
Bellah, R., 129–31, 158
bodily discharges and cultural boundaries, 94–95
Buddhism, 31–35, 49, 52–54, 65, 69, 71–72, 78, 108; on environment, 69; on evil and suffering, 65; on legitimacy of war, 71–72; relationship of, to grid/group scheme, 108; on status of women, 78

Callois, R., 75–76
caste system, 51–54
Christ, divinity of, 38–39, 61, 150
Christianity, 31–35, 38–43, 47–48, 59–69, 72–80, 109–11, 117–44, 150–51; on environment, 66–69; on evil and suffering, 59–65; on legitimacy of war, 72–74; relationship of, to grid/group scheme, 109–11; relationship of, to origins of science, 67–68; on status of women, 78–80; in United States, 117–44
civil religion, 113–44, 157–59; conflict of, with traditional religion, 127–29, 142–44; features of American, 131–44; God in, 129–30; separation of church and state as related to, 109–17, 140–41
civility as feature of civil religion, 131–34
Covenant, The, 35–37
Cuddihy, J. M., 132, 158

dancing, place of, in Christianity, 81–82, 154
denominations, historical significance of, in Christianity, 118–23
detachment, notion of, 49–50, 70–71
dietary assumptions, current, 93–94, 155
Douglas, M., 4, 84, 87–108, 131, 147–48, 155–56; on the Abominations of Leviticus, 87–94
Durkheim, 83, 87, 151

economic models and religion. *See* religion, and economic models
ego line, 102–3, 108
environment, religious attitudes toward, 66–70
evil, 105–7; problem of, 59–66; relationship of, to sin, etc., 105–7

features of American civil religion, 131–44
Freud, S., 64
functionalism and religion, 3, 18–19, 25, 147, 149

Galton, F., his "proof" of lack of efficacy of prayer, 11–12, 146
Gandhi, M., 70–71
Girard, R., his account of the origin of religion, 145, 148–49
grid. *See* grid and group
grid and group, 85–111; definition of grid, 98–99, 155–56; definition of group, 97–98, 155–56; relationships of, 96–100; relationships of major religions to, 108–9; relationships of societies to, 100–105; as used to chart history of religions in United States, 109–11, 122–28, 141–44
group. *See* grid and group
guilt, 105–7

Hammond, P. E., 130
Harris, M., on prohibition of swine flesh, 91–92
hell, 57, 62–63
Herberg, W., 121
hierarchies, segmented. *See* segmented hierarchies
Hinduism, 31–35, 48–52, 65, 69–71, 77–78, 108; on environment, 69; on evil and suffering, 65; on legitimacy of war, 70–71; relationship of, to grid/group scheme, 108; on status of women, 77–78
Holocaust, The, 61

ideology, 125–27
imitation of Christ, 61–62
inconsistency as a virtue of ideology, 125–27, 141–43
individuality: as feature of civil religion, 133–36; in Buddhism and Hinduism, 49–50
Islam, 31–35, 43–46, 63–64, 68–69, 74, 80–81, 92, 109; on environment, 68–69; on evil and suffering, 63–64; on legitimacy of war, 74; pig prohibition of, 92; relationship of, to grid/group scheme, 109; on status of women, 80–81

jihad, 74
Judaism, 31–39, 42–44, 47–48, 59–61, 68–69, 72, 78, 87–94, 120, 150; on environment, 68–69; on evil and suffering, 59–61; on legitimacy of war, 72; pig prohibition of, 87–92; relationship of, to grid/group scheme, 108–9; some associated conceptual boundaries of, 87–94; on status of women, 78

Kierkegaard, S., 16, 147
Kolakowski, L., his argument from truth to transcendence, 16–17
Kuhn, T. S., 12, 146–47

Leviticus, Abominations of, 87–94
Luckmann, T., 3, 145

Mariolatry, 79–80
Marxism: as religion, 31–35, 43, 46–48, 65–69, 74–76, 109, 137, 142–43, 151–52; on environment, 67–69; on evil and suffering, 64–65; on legitimacy of war, 74–75; relationship of, to grid/group scheme, 109; on status of women, 76, 151
miracles as evidence for Christianity, 38–39
Moses, 37, 45, 61
Muhammad, 43–45, 61, 151

orientalism, 69

original sin, 41

pastoralism, influence of, on Judaism, 34–35

problem of evil, 59–66; logical status of, in Christianity, 13–14, 62

Protestantism, 120–24, 135

public knowledge, as feature of civil religion, 139–40

Quran, relationship of, to earlier texts, 45–46, 151

ranking, as related to hierarchy, 137–38

rationality of religion, 10–14

religion: civil, *see* civil religion; defined, 24–26, 46, 57–58; and economic models, 19; as integrating society, 3; rationality of, 10–14; as reflecting society, 58, 83–84, 87–111, 117, 145; and science, their relationship, 5–16

religious institutions and religion, 118–24

representation in Judaism, 36–37, 150

scapegoating as related to individuality, 134–35

science: as feature of civil religion, 139–47; as related to religion, 5–16, 67–68, 85–86

secularization, 3, 19–20, 26, 119–22

segmented hierarchies as features of civil religion, 136–39, 158

shame, 105–7

sin, 105–7; and evil, relationship of, 62, 105–7

snot, 94–95

suffering, distribution of, 59–60

Tantra, status of women in, 77–78

toleration in American religion, 123–24

transcendence of God in Christianity, 40–41, 64

travel as similar to conversion, 23

Trinity, doctrine of The, 38–40

Turin, Shroud of, 12, 146

unity of science, doctrine of, 9

utilitarian individualism, 114, 130–31, 135–36, 141–42

veil and status of women, 80–81, 154

war, legitimacy of, 70–76

witchcraft, 21–22

Wittgenstein, L., on forms of life, 11, 148

women, social status of, 76–82